Herbs, Spices & Flavorings

by Doris McFerran Townsend

ANOTHER BESTSELLING VOLUME FROM HPBOOKS

Publishers: Bill and Helen Fisher; Executive Editor: Rick Bailey; Editorial Director: Helen Fisher; Editors: Faye Levy, Carroll Latham; Art Director: Don Burton; Book Design: Dana Martin; Food Stylist: Carol Peterson; Photography: George de Gennaro Studios

Published by HPBooks
P.O. Box 5367, Tucson, AZ 85703 602/888-2150
ISBN 0-89586-192-0 Library of Congress Catalog Card Number: 82-83338
©1982 Fisher Publishing Inc. Printed in U.S.A.

Cover photo: Clockwise from top: Chervil Butter, page 111; Rosemary in Olive Oil, see box on page 31; Hot Snap-Bean Salad, page 24; Cheese & Basil Bubbles, page 26.

Doris M. Townsend has written over 20 cookbooks, including *Cheese Cookery,* published by HPBooks. For many years Doris was editor-in-chief of a New York publishing house that specialized in cookbooks. Food styling, recipe development and testing, demonstrating new food products, hosting a radio talk show and writing advertising copy have all been part of her varied and rich experience.

Doris learned some of her seasoning magic while visiting among Amish and Mennonite friends in Pennsylvania. As a young person she was impressed by the old home-style cooking of relatives at Hidden Valley Farm in Minnesota. From these memories, she has incorporated the enchanting names and exciting recipes using seasoning experienced years ago.

In this book, Doris teaches you how to season food using herbs, spices and flavorings. You'll find practical dishes for every day and fabulous party recipes. Experienced and inexperienced cooks will enjoy using this easy guide to seasonings. The handy chart on pages 8 and 9 tells you what to use with any kind of food. Recipes using the various herbs, spices and flavorings are listed together in the index.

Herbs, Spices & Flavorings

The remarkable properties of herbs and spices have been appreciated by nearly every civilization since ancient times. According to historians, herbs were used by early civilizations as long ago as 3000 B.C. The Assyrians, Egyptians, Greeks and Romans all used herbs in a number of different ways. The ancients regarded herbs as being endowed with numerous almost-magical properties which made them valuable in cooking, medicines, cosmetics, perfumes, dyes and embalming. Herbs even had a place in that most famous of all gardens—the Garden of Eden.

The popularity of herbs was not limited to the East. Beautiful formal herb gardens were found in the grounds of every English monastery and castle during the Middle Ages. The garden was usually located close to the kitchen so the cook had easy access to fresh herbs to add to his pot.

The aromatic qualities of herbs made them valued as a means to flavor and preserve foods. This sought-after property comes from the essential oils of the plant. The application of heat encourages the release of these oils and their flavors are readily absorbed by food they are cooked with. When you add fresh or dried herbs to your dishes, it is always a good idea to crush the herb in the palm of your hand to promote the release of these flavorful oils.

In Europe, as in earlier eastern civilizations, herbs were not prized for their culinary uses alone. Their medicinal properties were described at length in several sturdy volumes in the sixteenth, seventeenth and eighteenth centuries. Among the notable authors of these *herbals* were John Gerard, John Parkinson, Nicholas Culpeper and Elizabeth Blackwell. Their scholarly writings make fascinating reading today. It is obvious from these works that the physicians of the day were also the first botanists. A thorough knowledge of the healing and soothing properties of plants was an essential part of the primitive science of medicine.

The European settlers who came to the New World in the seventeenth century cultivated herbs as they had done at home. In their journals they noted that the Indians made similar use of native herbs particularly in herbal teas and therapeutic mixtures.

Spices have an even more romantic history than herbs, although the histories of both are frequently entwined. Spices have been highly prized and bitterly fought over for centuries.

The first masters of the spice trade were the Arabs who controlled the routes as far back as 1700 B.C. Frequent references to spices, such as myrrh and cinnamon, appear in the Old Testament. It is clear from the descriptions that spices were regarded as luxury items. The geographical source of the spices was always kept as a guarded secret by the Arab traders. Consequently, when Europeans came to know and prize spices in about 900 A.D., finding the source and controlling the trade became the objective of every ruling monarch.

Christopher Columbus was not able to add the discovery of the spice islands to his achievements despite repeated efforts. Five years after Columbus' final unsuccessful attempt, Vasco da Gama did locate the source of the treasured spices in the East Indies. As a result, control of the trade passed to Spain and Portugal. The spice trade continued to be a source of military conflict between the various European countries. Power passed first to the Dutch and eventually to the British. The British Empire was founded on command of the spice trade and the creation of the East India Company in 1600.

Throughout the centuries, spices have been used for purposes similar to herbs. Ginger gave its distinctive flavor to the first gingerbread—a great favorite with the Greeks and Romans. Many other spices were key ingredients in healing potions and perfumed oils.

The popularity of both herbs and spices is on the rise again today for several reasons. More and more people are enjoying good cooking. And since flavor is a vital component of good food, herbs and spices are called upon increasingly by the creative cook. In recent years, the addition of salt has been our chief method of seasoning food. A new awareness of the detrimental effects on our health of high sodium consumption has lead many people to search for a low-sodium seasoning alternative. This is where herbs and spices come into their own. They can provide whatever flavor intensity the cook desires. A more widespread familiarity with international cuisines has also focused our attention on herbs and spices. It is often the addition of a particular herb or spice that gives a dish its ethnic identity.

Indoors and out, mankind's favorite pastime is eating. Without salt and the dozens of flavoring agents we have discovered and learned to use over many generations, all that beautiful food would be flat and have a sameness very disappointing to our palates.

Chief among the rules that govern the use of flavoring and seasoning agents is this: Restrain yourself—a little goes a long way. A little salt brings out the flavor of a dish; too much salt makes it bitter and inedible. A little of a spice or herb, a small portion of juice or peel, a modicum of extract, a touch of onion—all these give zest and bring a good dish to perfection. But, an excess of anything is overpowering.

We intensify the taste of food or add a touch of complementary flavor in many ways. The simplest of these methods is adding a flavoring to a mixture before, during or after cooking. This flavoring can be an appropriate spice, herb, extract, seasoned oil or vinegar, grated peel, or whatever will enhance the essential goodness of the dish. We incorporate garlic, onions and sweet and hot peppers. We compound spices and herbs, judiciously combining several into a compatible blend to use in sweet or savory dishes. Sometimes we incorporate basic beverages—tea, coffee, chocolate, wine, beer, liquor—into a mixture for rewarding flavor. Experiment with the following techniques and find new ways of enhancing the flavor of your favorite dishes.

Marinating is a technique in which meats and poultry, and sometimes vegetables, are immersed in a liquid. The liquid, or marinade, combines an acid—citrus juice or wine—and a fat, usually oil, with onions, garlic, herbs, spices or other flavorings. Marinating not only seasons the food, but acts as a *tenderizer* as well. To reinforce the seasoning, the marinating liquid is often used as a *baste* for the food during the cooking process.

Saucing stands on its own as a seasoning technique. Variations on the sauce theme number in the hundreds, but there are a few outstanding basics that every good home cook can rely on. Well-seasoned white sauces, *béchamels* and *veloutés* add creamy richness to foods. The many variations that can be made widen the cook's horizons. Other sauces, such as *hollandaise,* can lift simple dishes to elegance. And where would we be without savory tomato sauces in such great variety?

Homemade stocks form the basis of many excellent soups and sauces and offer a cooking medium far superior to water. Commercial sauces are available to add their particular pungency to many kinds of foods: Worcestershire—the sauce of many uses—soy sauce and hot red- or green-pepper sauce are only a few.

Dressing, for salads or similar mixtures to be served as main dishes or side dishes, is an important flavoring technique. Beginning with simple vinaigrette, often called *French dressing,* the field of dressings expands in all directions. There are old-fashioned boiled dressings, cheese dressings, nut dressings and fruit-salad dressings.

Basic to dressings are vinegar and oil. *Seasoned vinegars and oils* yield an even wider range of flavors than their plain relatives. They also have culinary uses outside of dressings. Many seasoned oils and vinegars can be prepared at home, or may be purchased in gourmet stores or gourmet sections of supermarkets.

Breading and *batter-dipping* are employed to protect foods to be fried, while giving them extra flavor.

Dredging and *dusting* are simple ways to cover foods with seasoned flour or sweet foods with flavored sugar.

Larding and *barding* are used mainly to combat

Medley of Herbs

1. Jerusalem artichoke (Sunchoke)
2. Anise
3. Marjoram
4. Oregano
5. Thyme
6. Garlic Blossom
7. Society Garlic Blossom
8. Sage (Dried)
9. Savory
10. Chamomile
11. Rosemary
12. Peppermint
13. Mint
14. Bay
15. Cardamom Pods
16. Marigold
17. Cinnamon sticks
18. Woodruff
19. Sage (Fresh)

dryness in meats, but also to season them. Larding consists of threading long thin strips of fat—plain or seasoned with herbs and garlic—through the meat. It requires a special tool, a larding needle. Barding is even simpler. It consists of laying thin pieces of fat on the surface of the meat and securing them in place with picks or twine.

Tucking is a meat-seasoning procedure. To tuck a leg of lamb, cut half-inch-deep slits about 1-1/2 inches apart over the surface of the meat and slip a sliver of garlic and a piece of rosemary into each.

Use of *mirepoix* is another meat-seasoning trick. A layer of vegetables, such as minced garlic and snipped parsley or a mélange of chopped onions, carrots and turnips, is placed in the bottom of a roasting pan. The meat is set on top. In a relatively low-temperature oven, the vegetables send up flavor-laden steam to bathe the meat as it cooks. Later, the vegetables can be pureed and returned to the meat drippings in the pan to form the base of a marvelous gravy.

Stuffing has two virtues—when well-seasoned, it adds flavor and extends the volume of the dish. Stuffing for holiday turkey, duck or goose uses herbs, spices, giblets, fruits, nuts, rice and potatoes. These are examples of stuffing at its best.

Sometimes a little something on the side is just what's needed to add grace to a meal. This is where *accompaniments* shine. Unusual homemade jams, jellies, preserves, ketchups, relishes and chutneys lift so-so dishes to a higher level. Homemade seasoned sweet and savory butters, toppings and spreads make everyday dishes into one-of-a-kind triumphs.

So it goes. A bit of this, a dab of that, and food becomes not just a meal, but a gustatory delight. Exploration of new seasoning and flavoring techniques pleases both cook and diners—for no one is ever quite satisfied with sameness. The chapters that follow can teach you new tricks and lead you into experiments on your own. Your home will be rich with the aroma of truly good cooking. Your table will be a treasure house of wonderful adventures in eating.

Seasoning Tools & Gadgets

Before you go on a gadget-buying spree, ask yourself: Is this tool really going to help me in the kitchen? Will it be used often enough to justify the storage space it will take? Is it easy to operate? Easy to clean? Sturdily constructed? Will a blender, food processor or knife do the job satisfactorily? If you can answer "yes" to all but the last question, you'll probably enjoy having and using some or all of these tools.

Pressing, Mashing, Bruising—A *garlic press* is one of the more useful gadgets. Look for the kind that comes apart and is dishwasher-safe. Some garlic presses are virtually impossible to clean thoroughly. Also useful is the combination of *mortar and pestle*. Besides serving the purposes of mashing, bruising and powdering, they are attractive additions to the kitchen. Again, look for ease of cleaning. Pottery and ceramic are easy to clean. Wood tends to hold flavors. Metal, except for stainless steel, may discolor the food or give it a metallic flavor. Herbs that are purchased dried in the leaf variety can be pulverized with a mortar and pestle, but your fingers will do just as well.

Grinding and Grating—Most cooks are familiar with *pepper grinders* which reduce peppercorns to a coarse or fine powder. *Salt grinders,* used to grind sea and other large-grained salt, are nearly as familiar. *Nutmeg and allspice grinders* grate the whole spice in the same fashion. *Nutmeg graters* are small versions of other kitchen graters which come in a wide variety of shapes and sizes. Most will grate citrus peel, but small porcelain *citrus graters,* made for this purpose, do the job well.

Spice and *seed grinders* look like small versions of grandma's meat grinder. One brand of spices packs the spice in its own grinder-topped box. This is convenient, but it makes the spice considerably more expensive.

Shredding and Stripping—Most kitchen graters do not have holes small enough to shred citrus peel. It can be done successfully with a small sharp knife and unlimited patience. A *citrus zester,* a knife-shaped gadget with four small holes instead of a blade, does the task beautifully. It shreds off only the *zest*—the oil and flavor-rich part of the peel—leaving the tough, bitter white membrane behind. A *citrus stripper* separates zest from membrane, producing long curls or twists of zest.

Juicing—For limes, a *lime juicer,* much like an enlarged garlic press, does an efficient job of juicing. For small amounts of juice, a *lemon juicer,* a plastic tube with a snap-on cover, can be pressed into a lemon. When the lemon is squeezed, small amounts of juice come out the far end. Unless you are a devoted gadget nut, this falls into the more-trouble-than-it's-worth category. A *hand reamer* is rather like an old-fashioned darning ball with grooves. The cut-side of a lemon, orange or lime is pressed and turned on the grooves to extract all or part of the juice. These were made of wood in Colonial times, but now can be had in heavy glass or dishwasher-safe plastic.

Chopping and Snipping—*Onion choppers* and *nut choppers* are widely available. In both, the food is placed in a small hopper at the top, a crank is turned and the chopped food falls into a glass container beneath the chopper. Or, you may feel that the old way is the best way, and employ a wooden *chopping bowl* with a double-bladed *rocking chopper. Blenders* and *food processors* will also chop. However, unless handled expertly, they often chop too fine, giving a chewed-up texture. Sharp, sturdy *kitchen scissors* are best for cutting up herbs. You can snip them into pieces of whatever size you want, without bruising or mashing the herb. A *parsley wheel* has round blades that roll over herbs. It works reasonably well, but scissors are better.

Slicing and Dicing—Good *knives,* well sharpened, are really all that are needed. The *food processor* will both dice and slice, but often it's not worth the clean-up trouble when only a small amount of diced or sliced food is needed. An *egg slicer*—preferably metal—is useful for turning out neatly sliced hard-cooked eggs. The same is true of an *egg wedger,* which will also cut small vegetables, such as radishes or sections of carrot, into wedges for garnishing. A *tomato slicer,* also used for onions, resembles a comb with long, sharp metal teeth. The vegetable is impaled on it and sliced by a knife inserted between the teeth. You'll do as well with a sharp serrated knife for tomatoes and a sharp plain blade for onions.

When you work with hot peppers, whatever tool you use, wear *rubber* or *plastic gloves* to protect your fingers from the painful burns these pretty, innocent-looking vegetables can give you.

A *pineapple prince* does the messy job of peeling and coring a pineapple in one process, and is a worthwhile investment. An *apple wedger* cuts apples and pears into neat wedges and cores them at the same time, but a knife does as well.

All of these, and doubtless other tools and gadgets that don't immediately spring to mind, are available in housewares departments and kitchen specialty shops. You can also get them by mail from most of the sources on page 156.

Learn to grow herbs. An excellent source is *Herbs: How to Select, Grow and Enjoy,* by Norma Jean Lathrop and published by HPBooks. It will instruct you on how to plant, grow and harvest herbs—indoors and outdoors.

Fresh & Dried Herbs, left to right: Sweet Basil, Marjoram, Savory, Oregano, Sage, Tarragon, Thyme.

Herbs: What Goes With What

	Appetizers	Soups & Chowders	Salads	Fish & Shellfish	Poultry & Game	Meats	Sauces	Eggs & Cheese	Vegetables
Basil	cheese spreads seafood cocktails tomato juice	fish chowders minestrone pea spinach tomato vegetable	chicken cucumber fruit green seafood tomato	crab halibut mackerel salmon shrimp tuna	chicken duck rabbit turkey venison	beef lamb liver pork sausage veal	butter orange sauce for game spaghetti chili tomato	cheese soufflé cheese spread omelets rarebits scrambled eggs	beans eggplant onions peas squash tomatoes
Bay Leaf	poaching liquid for shellfish pickles	bean beef stock bouillabaisse chicken-corn oxtail & vegetable	aspic beef	poaching liquid for shellfish halibut salmon	fricasseed chicken or rabbit	pot roast lamb or beef kabobs stews tongue tripe	barbecue curry spaghetti chili sour cream tomato		beets carrots potatoes stewed tomatoes
Chervil	avocado dip cheese dip and spread canapés butter	chicken or beef stock vegetable	beet cole slaw cucumber fruit green tomato	poaching liquid for fillets	stuffing for all game	stews seasonings for ground meats	barbecue butter cream spaghetti sour cream tartar	cream cheese spread deviled eggs omelets rarebits soufflés	beets eggplant peas potatoes spinach tomatoes
Dillweed	cheese dip and spread seafood cocktails & spreads deviled eggs	bean borscht chicken fish & shellfish chowder pea tomato	beet cole slaw potato seafood mixed vegetable	halibut salmon shrimp sole	creamed chicken chicken pie	beef corned beef lamb pork sweetbreads veal	cream sauce for fish tartar	cottage cheese omelets scrambled eggs	beans beets cabbage celery parsnips potatoes
Marjoram	savory butters cheese dip & spread stuffed mushrooms pizza-style canapés	chicken noodle clam chowder onion oyster bisque spinach tomato	asparagus chicken fruit green seafood	clams crab sauté creamed tuna halibut salmon	chicken duck goose rabbit turkey venison	beef pork pot roast sausage stews veal	brown cream chili sour cream tomato	omelets rarebits scrambled eggs soufflés	brussels sprouts carrots onions peas spinach zucchini
Oregano	avocado dip cheese spread stuffed mushrooms mushroom spreads tomato juice	bean minestrone mushroom onion tomato vegetable	avocado white bean 3-bean green potato seafood tomato	clams creamed lobster or crab shrimp	chicken guinea hen stuffing for pheasant	ground beef lamb liver sausage stews veal	barbecue brown mushroom spaghetti chili tomato	soft-cooked eggs cheese soufflé omelets rarebits scrambled eggs	broccoli cabbage lentils mushrooms onions tomatoes

Left to right: Cinnamon, Nutmeg, Allspice, Cloves, Pepper, Red Pepper, Vanilla Bean and Vanilla Extract.

	Appetizers	Soups & Chowders	Salads	Fish & Shellfish	Poultry & Game	Meats	Sauces	Eggs & Cheese	Vegetables
Parsley	avocado dip savory butters canapés cheese dip & spread	chicken or beef stock vegetable	fruit green potato seafood vegetable	poaching liquid	stuffings for all poultry & game	stews ground meat garnish for steaks & chops	barbecue butter cream spaghetti sour cream tartar	cream cheese spread deviled eggs omelets rarebits soufflés	carrots potatoes tomatoes
Peppermint	cranberry juice fruit salad & fruit cup garnishes	bean pea	fruit gelatin celery cole slaw green	shrimp prawns		ground beef ground lamb lamb stew roast lamb veal	cranberry currant mint	cream cheese spread	carrots peas potatoes spinach zucchini
Rosemary	fruit cup pickles	chicken fish chowders pea potato spinach turtle	fruit	poaching liquid for salmon & halibut broiled salmon	capon duck chicken quail rabbit	beef ham loaf lamb pork stews veal	barbecue brown butter cream salsa tomato	deviled eggs scrambled eggs soufflés	cauliflower cucumbers mushrooms peas potatoes spinach
Saffron	savory butters	bouillabaisse chicken & rice turkey	chicken fish & shellfish	baked sole & halibut		lamb or veal curry veal stew	cream sauce for fish curry sauces	cream cheese spreads scrambled eggs	vegetables & rice squash zucchini
Sage	sharp cheese spreads	chicken pea potato tomato turkey vegetable		baked sole & halibut poached salmon	chicken duck goose rabbit turkey stuffings	beef lamb pork sausage stews	brown butter cheese sauce for eggs	cottage cheese creamed eggs	carrots eggplant lima beans onions peas tomatoes
Savory	cheese spreads liver pâté deviled egg vegetable or tomato juice	bean chicken chowders lentil pea vegetable	white bean green potato tomato vegetable	halibut shrimp sole crab salmon	chicken duck squab turkey venison stuffings	kidney lamb shanks meatloaf pot roast spareribs veal cutlets	butter for steak butter for fish horseradish	deviled eggs omelets scrambled eggs soufflés	artichokes asparagus beans lentils rice sauerkraut
Tarragon	cheese spreads liver pâté seafood deviled egg tomato juice	bean chicken mushroom pea tomato	chicken cole slaw egg fruit fish & shellfish	salmon crab halibut lobster shrimp sole	chicken duck goose squab turkey	lamb pork chops pot roast stews sweetbreads veal	béarnaise mustard sour cream tartar vinaigrette	cottage cheese deviled eggs omelets scrambled eggs baked eggs	cauliflower celery root mushrooms potatoes spinach tomatoes
Thyme	liver pâté sauerkraut juice seafood cocktails & spreads	borscht clam chowder consommé gumbo pea vegetable	aspics beet chicken cole slaw tomato	cod & sole crab creamed tuna halibut scallops	chicken duck pheasant turkey stuffings	beef lamb pork veal variety meats	creole curry mustard spaghetti salsa tomato	cottage cheese deviled eggs omelets shirred eggs soufflés	asparagus beans beets carrots onions zucchini

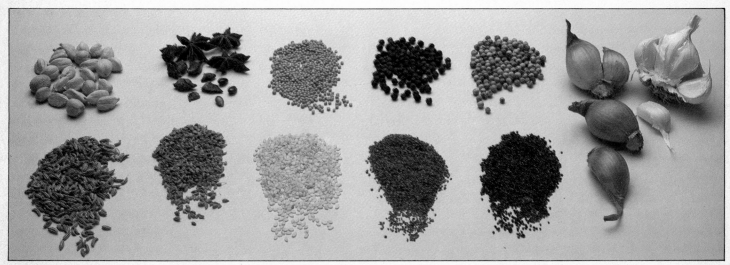

Top row: Cardamom Pods, Star Anise, Mustard, Black Peppercorns, White Peppercorns, Shallots, Garlic.
Bottom row: Fennel, Anise, Sesame, Celery, Poppy Seeds.

Spices

Spices are fragrant, aromatic, often pungent vegetable substances used to flavor food. They are usually grown in the tropics. Following is a list of the most often-used spices.

● *Allspice* is the berry of a warm-climate evergreen tree that will grow almost anywhere but only bears fruit in Jamaica, Guatemala, Honduras and Mexico. It smells and tastes like a mixture of cloves, cinnamon and nutmeg. Available as dried whole berries, ground and as an extract.

● *Cardamom,* fruit of a plant in the ginger family, is native to India. The flavor, unlike any other, is the principal spice in Danish pastry. Available as green or bleached pods, or ground.

● *Cinnamon* comes from the bark of an evergreen tree. It is known and used all over the world. Once it was burned as incense, made into a fragrant bath oil and used as an ingredient in love potions. Available ground, in sticks—technically called *quills*—and as an extract.

● *Cloves* are the unopened flower buds of an evergreen tree native to the Moluccas, formerly called the Spice Islands. It was once the most costly of spices, over which wars were fought. Available whole or ground.

● *Coriander* is the seed of a plant whose leaves are used as an herb. The seed flavors frankfurters, is a component of curry powders and mixed pickling spices and is often used in baking. Available as whole seeds or ground.

● *Cumin* was once thought to ensure the happiness of a couple who carried it through their wedding. It is a component of both chili and curry powders. Use it to flavor pork or cheese dishes. Available as whole seeds or ground.

● *Ginger* was used as both an herb and a spice as long as 5,000 years ago, when the Greeks enjoyed a kind of gingerbread. Available as fresh whole or chopped root, ground, crystallized or candied, and preserved in syrup.

● *Nutmeg* and *mace* are both from the same tropical tree. *Nutmeg* is the brown pit of the peach-like fruit; *mace* is the red lace network called *aril,* that covers the pit. Nutmeg is available whole, ground or as an extract. Mace is available ground, or as *blade mace,* which are pieces of dried aril.

● *Paprika* is a rosy-red pulverized pepper. It comes in three strengths: sweet, half-sweet and hot. This seasoning is used in larger quantities than most other spices. Besides adding flavor, paprika adds color to foods.

● *Pepper* is as widely known in all parts of the world as salt. Peppercorns come from a vine called *piper nigrum.* It grows in warm climates. Green peppercorns are picked before they are ripe. They are available in brine or vinegar and air- or freeze-dried. Black peppercorns are dried mature berries. Matured still further, peppercorns become pink, then white. They may be purchased whole or in fine, medium or coarse grinds.

● *Saffron,* the most costly spice today, is the dried stigmas of a crocus. It imparts flavor and rich, golden color to many foods. Available ground and as whole dried stigmas or threads.

● *Turmeric,* a root of the ginger family, is a component of curry powders. It imparts both delicious flavor and rich golden color to foods. It is available only in ground form.

Today, we use spices in every kind of food relying on their pungency to enhance other flavors or to stand alone.

Summertime Pea Soup

Easy to make for a warm-weather lunch or for the start of a more substantial meal.

1 (10-oz.) pkg. frozen peas
1 large iceberg lettuce leaf
1/4 teaspoon salt
1/8 teaspoon ground white pepper

1 cup Chicken Stock, page 98,
  or canned chicken broth
1/4 teaspoon ground cardamom
1 cup half and half

Into blender, break frozen peas in chunks. Tear lettuce into 4 pieces and add to peas. Add salt, pepper and stock or broth. Process at medium speed until pureed. Add cardamom and half and half. Process at low speed until well blended. Refrigerate soup until serving time. Serve cold or hot. To heat, pour into a medium saucepan. Bring soup to serving temperature over low heat; do not boil. Taste for seasoning. Makes 4 servings.

Golden Spiced Chicken Breasts

The blandness of white meat disappears when chicken is seasoned this way.

1 garlic clove, minced
1/2 teaspoon ground turmeric
1/2 teaspoon ground ginger
1/4 teaspoon salt
1/8 teaspoon crushed saffron threads
1/3 cup olive oil
6 chicken-breast halves, skinned, boned

2 tablespoons butter or margarine
3/4 cup sliced onion
About 1-1/2 cups Chicken Stock,
  page 98, or canned chicken broth
3/4 cup whipping cream
3-1/2 cups hot cooked rice
3 tablespoons snipped fresh parsley

Combine garlic, turmeric, ginger, salt and saffron; mix well. Add 1/4 cup olive oil; mix until blended. Coat chicken-breast halves with this mixture, rubbing into the meat. Refrigerate several hours or overnight. In a large skillet, heat remaining olive oil with butter or margarine. Add onion. Cook over low heat until soft but not browned. Add chicken pieces and enough stock or broth to cover chicken. Cover and simmer until chicken is tender and opaque, about 25 minutes. Remove chicken; keep warm. Increase heat to medium-high; cook broth until reduced to about 3/4 cup. Add cream; stir to blend. Continue to cook until mixture is further reduced and very slightly thickened. Taste sauce for seasoning. Spread rice on a heated serving platter. Top with chicken. Spoon sauce over chicken. Sprinkle with parsley. Makes 6 servings.

Lamb-Yam Casserole Jamaica-Style

Tender lamb with a glorious mélange of spice-scented vegetables and bananas.

2-1/2 lbs. boneless lamb shoulder,
   cut in 1-1/2-inch cubes
2 medium onions, chopped
2 garlic cloves, partially crushed
1-1/2 teaspoons ground coriander
1 teaspoon dried leaf oregano, crumbled
1/2 teaspoon ground cumin
1/4 teaspoon ground ginger
1/4 teaspoon ground cinnamon
2 tablespoons soy sauce

1 cup hot water
6 medium carrots, peeled
3 lbs. medium yams or sweet potatoes,
   peeled, halved lengthwise if large
3 completely green bananas
1 (14- to 16-oz.) can whole plum tomatoes,
   undrained
1/4 cup all-purpose flour
Salt and ground black pepper to taste

Preheat oven to 425F (220C). Place lamb in a large shallow casserole or in a 13'' x 9'' baking pan. Sprinkle with onions and garlic. In a small bowl, combine coriander, oregano, cumin, ginger and cinnamon. Sprinkle over meat. Drizzle soy sauce over meat. Slowly add water to pan. Cover tightly with a lid or foil. Bake in preheated oven 1-1/4 hours. While meat is cooking, cut carrots into thick diagonal slices. Stir carrots into meat mixture. Arrange yams or sweet potatoes around meat. Replace cover and bake 15 minutes longer. Peel bananas and cut into chunks about the same size as carrot pieces; set banana pieces aside. Drain 1/2 cup tomato liquid into a small bowl. Set aside tomatoes and remaining liquid. Stir flour into bowl of tomato liquid until smooth. Remove casserole from oven. Stir flour mixture into casserole carefully but thoroughly. Add bananas and tomatoes with remaining liquid. Stir gently. Replace cover and continue baking until meat and vegetables are tender, 30 to 45 minutes. Season to taste with salt and pepper. Makes 6 servings.

Perfection Onion Rings

Forget breading, forget fritter batter—sometimes simpler is better!

6 large Bermuda or Spanish onions,
   cut in 1/4-inch slices
Milk
1 cup all-purpose flour

1/4 teaspoon ground white pepper
1/4 teaspoon sweet paprika
Oil for deep-frying
Salt

Separate onion slices into rings; place in a large bowl. Add milk to cover. Let stand at room temperature 1 hour. In a pie plate or other shallow pan, combine flour, white pepper and paprika; set aside. Pour oil for deep-frying 1-1/2 inches deep into a deep-fat fryer or electric skillet. Heat oil to 375F (190C). At this temperature, a 1-inch cube of bread will turn golden brown in 40 seconds. Remove onion rings from milk one at a time, shaking off excess milk. Dip into flour mixture to coat on all sides. Carefully lower a few coated rings into hot oil. Fry, a few at a time, until golden brown. Drain on paper towels. Sprinkle lightly with salt. Serve as soon as possible; keep fried rings hot in a 200F (95C) oven while frying remaining rings. Makes 4 to 6 servings.

Martinique-Style Spicy Pork

Use this homemade cold-cut in sandwiches or serve thin slices with potato salad.

1 (5-lb.) pork loin roast, boned	2 carrots, peeled, sliced
1 teaspoon salt	1 large onion, sliced
1/2 teaspoon ground black pepper	10 whole allspice
1/2 teaspoon sugar	8 black peppercorns
1/2 teaspoon ground allspice	1 qt. water
6 whole cloves	

Cut away and discard all visible fat from pork. Combine salt, ground pepper, sugar and ground all-spice. Rub into all surfaces of meat. Using cotton kitchen string, tie meat into a compact roll, securing string both lengthwise and crosswise at 2- to 3-inch intervals. Stud meat with cloves. Place in a 5-quart pot. Add remaining ingredients. Bring to a boil. Cover; reduce heat to low. Simmer 1-1/2 hours, turning meat twice during cooking time. Remove from heat. Place a heavy plate or pie pan directly on meat and weight heavily with a brick or 2 large, heavy cans of food. Refrigerate overnight. Remove meat from broth. Cut and remove string. Wrap meat in plastic wrap and refrigerate up to 1 week. To serve, cut in thin slices. Makes 10 to 12 servings.

How to Make Martinique-Style Spicy Pork

1/Tie meat into a compact roll, securing both lengthwise and crosswise at 2- to 3-inch intervals.

2/To serve, remove string; refrigerate meat until thoroughly cooled. Slice and use to make sandwiches.

Rosy Eggs-in-a-Pickle

Fine as an appetizer or snack—or serve at a patio buffet, on a picnic or in lunch boxes.

1 (16-oz.) can sliced beets
12 hard-cooked eggs, shelled
3/4 cup cider vinegar
1/2 cup sugar
2 tablespoons salt

1/2 teaspoon coarsely
 ground black pepper
1/8 teaspoon ground allspice
6 whole cloves

Drain liquid from beets into a 1-quart saucepan. Place eggs and drained beets in a large jar or heat-proof bowl; set aside. Stir vinegar into beet juice. Stir in sugar, salt, pepper, allspice and cloves. Bring to a boil over high heat, stirring constantly. Pour hot beet-juice mixture over eggs and beets. Cover and refrigerate 24 hours or up to 2 weeks. To serve, use a slotted spoon to remove as many eggs and beets as needed at one time. Drain well. Makes 12 servings.

Mediterranean Carrot Salad

Slightly sweet, delicately spicy, this makes a delectable, unusual meat accompaniment.

2 lbs. carrots, peeled
2 garlic cloves, peeled, halved
1/2 teaspoon ground cumin
1/4 teaspoon ground cinnamon
1 teaspoon sweet paprika

1/8 teaspoon red (cayenne) pepper
2 tablespoons lemon juice
1/4 teaspoon sugar
1/4 teaspoon salt
3 tablespoons olive oil

In a medium saucepan, place whole carrots and halved garlic. Cover with cold water. Bring to a boil over high heat. Reduce heat to medium-low. Cook until carrots are barely tender. Drain; discard garlic. Cut carrots into thin slices. Place in a serving dish. In a small bowl, combine cumin, cinnamon, paprika and red pepper. Stir to blend. Stir in lemon juice, sugar and salt. Pour over carrots. Refrigerate at least 2 hours. Just before serving, pour olive oil evenly over carrot mixture. Makes 6 servings.

Rice Madras

Seasonings and fruit turn plain boiled rice into a delightful dish.

3 cups Chicken Stock, page 98,
 or canned chicken broth
2 tablespoons butter or margarine
1/2 teaspoon salt

2 teaspoons ground turmeric
1-1/2 cups uncooked long-grain white rice
1/2 cup finely chopped apple
1/4 cup dried currants

In a medium saucepan, bring stock or broth to a boil. Stir in butter or margarine, salt, turmeric and rice. Bring again to a boil; cover. Reduce heat to low. Simmer, without removing cover, until rice is tender, about 20 minutes. Gently stir in apple and currants. Cover again and cook 2 minutes longer. Fluff with a fork. Serve immediately. Makes 6 to 8 servings.

Peppercorn Steak

This is the justly famous French Steak au Poivre.

1 (3-1/2-lb.) sirloin steak,	**1/4 cup olive oil or vegetable oil**
1-1/2 inches thick	**1/4 cup Beef Stock, page 98,**
3 tablespoons black peppercorns	**or canned beef broth**
Salt to taste	**2 tablespoons brandy or**
1/4 cup butter or margarine	**2 teaspoons red-wine vinegar**

Slash fat around edge of steak at 2-inch intervals to prevent steak from curling as it cooks. Place peppercorns in a plastic bag. Strike several times with a wooden mallet or rolling pin to crack. Rub half of cracked pepper into each side of steak, pushing pieces into meat with heel of your hand. Sprinkle lightly with salt to taste. Let meat stand at room temperature 20 minutes. In a large skillet, heat butter or margarine and oil over high heat. Add steak; quickly sear on each side. Reduce heat to medium. Cook 4 to 7 minutes on each side, depending on degree of doneness desired. Place steak on a warm serving platter. Discard all but 2 tablespoons liquid from skillet. Add stock or broth and brandy or vinegar to skillet. Bring to a boil; pour over steak. Serve immediately. Makes 4 to 5 servings.

Green-Peppercorn Chicken

An easy and elegant dish to serve with pride to family or guests.

4 large chicken-breast halves,	**1 cup whipping cream**
skinned, boned	**4 teaspoons drained canned**
Salt and white ground pepper	**green peppercorns (water pack)**
6 tablespoons butter or margarine	
1 cup Chicken Stock, page 98,	
or canned chicken broth	

Place chicken-breast halves between 2 pieces of waxed paper. Using a meat mallet or a rolling pin, pound chicken to flatten slightly. Sprinkle lightly with salt and white pepper. In a large skillet, melt 1/4 cup butter or margarine over medium heat. Sauté chicken pieces until tender and opaque, about 3 minutes on each side. Place on a platter; keep warm. Discard fat remaining in skillet. Pour stock or broth into skillet. Bring to simmering point over medium heat. Stirring with a whisk, slowly add cream. Bring to a slow boil. Cook until sauce is thickened and reduced in volume. Add peppercorns. Cook about 5 minutes longer until mixture lightly coats a spoon. Use a whisk to stir in remaining 2 tablespoons butter or margarine. Season to taste with salt and white pepper. Spoon sauce over chicken pieces; serve immediately. Makes 4 servings.

Save milk in which onions have soaked, page 12; refrigerate and tightly cover. Use as the base for a cream of spinach or mushroom soup.

Ginger-Braised Pork

Accompanied by rice or noodles and a green salad, this makes an easy, flavorful meal.

2 lbs. boneless lean pork from loin or
   shoulder, cut in 1-inch cubes
1/3 cup all-purpose flour
3 tablespoons vegetable oil
1/2 cup Chicken Stock, page 98,
   or canned chicken broth
1/2 cup water

1/4 cup soy sauce
2 tablespoons sherry
1/4 cup chopped onion
1 small garlic clove, minced
1-1/2 teaspoons sugar
1-1/2 teaspoons ground ginger
2 drops hot-pepper sauce

In a bag, shake pork cubes and flour together. In a large skillet, heat oil. Add floured pork; brown quickly over medium heat. Remove pork with a slotted spoon; set aside. Pour off and discard oil from skillet. Add remaining ingredients to skillet. Return pork cubes to skillet. Bring mixture to a boil. Reduce heat. Cover skillet. Simmer until pork is tender, 15 to 20 minutes. Serve immediately. Makes 6 servings.

Mount Vernon Ginger Biscuits

Today we call them cookies—and, as Washington did, we call them delicious.

1/2 cup butter or margarine,
   room temperature
1/4 cup vegetable shortening
1-1/3 cups sugar
1 egg
1/4 cup dark molasses

1-3/4 cups all-purpose flour
1 teaspoon baking soda
1 teaspoon ground cinnamon
1 teaspoon ground cloves
1 teaspoon ground ginger

In large bowl of electric mixer, cream butter or margarine and shortening until soft and fluffy. Slowly add 1 cup sugar, beating until light and fluffy. Beat in egg and molasses. In a medium bowl, combine flour, baking soda, cinnamon, cloves and ginger. Stir lightly to blend. Gradually stir into sugar mixture until blended. Cover and refrigerate 1 hour. Preheat oven to 375F (190C). Grease 2 large baking sheets. Pour remaining 1/3 cup sugar into a small dish. Roll chilled cookie dough between palms of your hands into 1-inch balls. Roll in sugar, then place on baking sheets about 3 inches apart. Bake in preheated oven until firm and lightly browned, 12 to 15 minutes. Cool 15 minutes on baking sheet, then place on racks to cool. Cookies can be stored up to 2 weeks in an airtight metal container at room temperature, or wrapped airtight and frozen. Makes about 40 cookies.

When preparing fresh herbs for cooking, cut off and discard heavy stems, which are often bitter. Using kitchen scissors, snip herb leaves to the size required by the recipe. If herbs are to be bruised or crushed, place leaves in a mortar or small bowl; crush with a pestle or the back of a heavy spoon.

Spiced Cream Twists

Serve for breakfast or brunch, as a snack, or as a not-too-sweet dessert.

4 cups all-purpose flour	**1 egg**
1 teaspoon salt	**2 egg yolks**
3/4 teaspoon ground mace	**1 cup dairy sour cream**
1 cup cold butter or margarine	**1/2 teaspoon vanilla extract**
1 (1/4-oz.) pkg. active dry yeast	**Sugar for work surface**
(1 tablespoon)	**1/4 teaspoon ground nutmeg**
1/4 cup warm water (110F, 45C)	**1/3 cup sugar**

In a large bowl, combine flour, salt and mace. Stir lightly to blend. With a pastry blender or 2 knives, cut in butter or margarine until coarse crumbs form; set aside. In a small bowl, stir yeast into warm water. Let stand until bubbly, about 10 minutes. In a medium bowl, beat together egg, egg yolks and sour cream until smooth. Stir in yeast mixture and vanilla. Stir egg mixture into flour mixture until thoroughly combined but not completely smooth. Cover and refrigerate 2 hours. Preheat oven to 375F (190C). Lightly sprinkle a clean flat surface with sugar. Turn dough out onto sugared surface; turn dough over. Use a rolling pin to roll dough into a a 12-inch square. Fold lefthand third of dough over center third. Fold righthand third over top to cover first folded section exactly. Turn dough 90 degrees to the right, so the open end of the last fold is away from you. Roll again into a 12-inch square, adding more sugar as required to keep dough from sticking to work surface and rolling pin. Repeat rolling, folding and turning 4 times. Roll dough once again to 12-inch square. Cut square in half. Cut each half crosswise into strips about 3/4 inch wide and 6 inches long. Combine nutmeg and 1/3 cup sugar. Sprinkle each strip of dough with nutmeg mixture. Twist each strip 4 times. Place on an ungreased baking sheet, 3 inches apart. Bake until very lightly browned, about 20 minutes. Cool on racks. Serve warm or completely cooled. Twists can be stored in an airtight bag or container at room temperature up to 2 days, or wrapped airtight and frozen. Makes about 24 twists.

Deviled Cashews

Once you start snacking on these, it will take all your willpower to stop!

3 tablespoons butter or margarine	**1/8 teaspoon sweet paprika**
1 lb. shelled raw cashews	**1/4 teaspoon red (cayenne) pepper**
1/8 teaspoon Worcestershire sauce	**1/8 teaspoon chili powder**
1-1/2 teaspoons salt	**1/8 teaspoon ground cumin**

In a large skillet, melt butter or margarine; add nuts. Stir over medium heat until golden brown, 3 to 5 minutes. Drain on paper towels. In a small bowl or cup, combine remaining ingredients. Stir to blend. Place drained nuts in a paper or plastic bag. Add salt mixture. Close neck of bag and shake well to coat nuts. Cool and serve, or store in a closed jar in a cool, dark place. Makes 1 pound.

Variations
Substitute almonds, pecans, filberts or a combination of nuts for cashews.

How to Make Spiced Cream Twists

1/Roll dough to a 12-inch square. Fold left third of dough over center. Fold right third of dough over center.

2/Turn dough 1/4 turn so open ends are to right and left of you. Repeat rolling, folding and turning 4 times.

3/Cut 12-inch square into two 12" x 6" rectangles. Cut each rectangle into 6" x 3/4" strips.

4/Sprinkle strips with nutmeg mixture. Twist each strip 4 times, then arrange on an ungreased baking sheet.

Gingery Lemon Sherbet

Cool and refreshing as any lemon dessert—but with the extra zing of ginger.

2/3 cup sugar
2 cups cold water
1-1/4 teaspoons unflavored gelatin
1/2 cup lemon juice
2 drops yellow food coloring, if desired

1/4 cup finely chopped candied ginger
2 egg whites
1/8 teaspoon salt
Fresh mint leaves, if desired

In a medium saucepan, combine sugar and 1-3/4 cups water. Bring to a boil over medium-high heat, stirring occasionally. Boil 10 minutes. While sugar mixture cooks, sprinkle gelatin over remaining 1/4 cup water. Let stand 3 to 4 minutes to soften. Remove sugar syrup from heat; stir in gelatin mixture until dissolved. Cool 5 minutes. Stir in lemon juice and yellow food coloring, if desired. Stir in ginger. In a medium bowl, beat egg whites until stiff but not dry. Beat in salt. Fold into lemon mixture. Spoon into undivided ice trays. Cover with foil and place in freezer for at least 4 hours. About 30 minutes before serving, place trays in refrigerator. Spoon slightly softened sherbet into dessert dishes. Garnish with mint leaves, if desired. Makes 4 servings.

Viennese Snowtop Coffee

Serve "mit Schlag"—with whipped cream—in place of a heavy dessert.

2 teaspoons Viennese Coffee Mix,
  see below
2/3 cup boiling water

1 tablespoon or dollop whipped cream
Grated semisweet chocolate

Viennese Coffee Mix:
1/2 cup instant coffee powder
1/2 cup packed light-brown sugar
1 tablespoon grated orange peel

2 teaspoons ground cinnamon
1 teaspoon ground allspice
1/2 teaspoon ground nutmeg

Prepare Viennese Coffee Mix. At serving time, place 2 teaspoons mix in a large coffee cup. Add boiling water. Stir until mixture dissolves. Top with 1 tablespoon or dollop whipped cream and a light dusting of grated chocolate. Makes 1 serving.

Viennese Coffee Mix:
In a medium bowl, combine all ingredients. Stir until blended. Spoon into a 2-cup container with a tight-fitting lid. Cover and store at room temperature up to 4 days or in refrigerator up to 1 month. Makes about 1-1/3 cups dry mix or 30 servings.

Although a spice rack may be attractive over the stove, this is the worst place to store spices and herbs. The heat dissipates the flavors. Store them in a cool closed cupboard.

Speculaas

These spicy cookie-press treats are a favorite of children in the Netherlands.

3/4 cup butter or margarine,
  room temperature
2 cups packed dark-brown sugar
2 eggs
1/3 cup light molasses
3 tablespoons brandy or apple juice
2 teaspoons cider vinegar
3-1/2 cups all-purpose flour

2 tablespoons ground cinnamon
2 teaspoons ground cardamom
2 teaspoons ground nutmeg
1/4 teaspoon ground cloves
1-1/2 teaspoons salt
1-1/2 teaspoons baking soda
About 1-1/4 cups blanched almonds,
  halved lengthwise

Grease a large baking sheet; set aside. In large bowl of electric mixer, cream butter or margarine and brown sugar until light and fluffy. Add eggs; beat 2 minutes. Add molasses, brandy or apple juice and vinegar; beat 3 minutes. In a medium bowl, combine flour, spices, salt and baking soda. Gradually add to egg mixture, beating after each addition until blended. Preheat oven to 375F (190C). Assemble cookie press as manufacturer directs, using the bar plate. Fill press with dough. Press dough onto prepared baking sheet to make 3-inch bars. Top each bar with 3 or 4 almond halves; then press a second layer of dough over almonds. Bake in preheated oven until cookies are lightly browned and edges are crisp, about 12 minutes. Cool on racks. Repeat with remaining dough. Cookies can be stored up to 2 weeks in an airtight metal container at room temperature, or wrapped airtight and frozen. Makes about 72 cookies.

Citrus & Spice Tea

Warm on a cold day, cool on a hot one—and so easy to make!

1/2 cup Citrus & Spice Tea Mix,
  see below
2 qts. boiling water

Thin lemon slices for garnish,
  if desired
Mint sprigs for garnish, if desired

Citrus & Spice Tea Mix:
1 cup orange-flavored breakfast
  beverage powder
1 teaspoon grated lemon peel
3/4 cup sugar

1/2 cup instant tea powder
1 teaspoon ground cinnamon
1/2 teaspoon ground cloves
1/2 teaspoon ground allspice

Prepare Citrus & Spice Tea Mix. Rinse a glass pitcher or earthenware pitcher with hot water. Place 1/2 cup tea mix in pitcher. Slowly add boiling water. Let stand 2 to 3 minutes. To serve, pour into large cups. Add lemon slice or mint sprig to each cup, if desired. Makes 6 to 8 servings.

Citrus & Spice Tea Mix:
In a medium bowl, combine all ingredients. Stir until blended. Spoon into a 2-1/2-cup container with a tight-fitting lid. Cover and store at room temperature up to 7 days or in refrigerator up to 3 months. Makes 2-1/4 cups dry mix. For a single serving, use 1 tablespoon mix.

Variation

Iced Citrus & Spice Tea: Brew as above, but reduce boiling water to 1 quart. Let cool; then add 2 cups cold water. Pour over ice cubes in tall drinking glasses.

Herbs

There was a time when every household had two gardens. One, the kitchen garden, supplied vegetables for cooking and "sallets." The other, a formal garden, supplied a feast for the eyes and flowers for the house.

Today, an herb garden or a sunny windowsill with potted plants offers great culinary rewards. Although we buy dried herbs whenever we wish, there is no denying that fresh herbs have better and more subtle flavor. Most supermarkets have a limited variety of herbs such as parsley, watercress, cilantro and dill. During the summer months you may find basil, mint, oregano or marjoram. It is easy to grow your own. You can raise herbs from seeds, but it is best to set out small plants. An excellent guide is HPBooks' *Herbs, How to Select, Grow and Enjoy,* by Norma Jean Lathrop.

The most widely used herbs are *basil, bay leaf, fresh coriander*—also called *Chinese* or *Mexican parsley* or *cilantro*—*dill, marjoram, mint, oregano, parsley, rosemary, sage, tarragon* and *thyme.* But there are many others. *Savory,* both summer and winter varieties, and *lovage* are old favorites being rediscovered by today's cooks. *Burnet,* with its cucumber-like flavor, is a welcome addition to a green salad. *Fennel* is used fresh as a vegetable. The seed and leaf are used for flavoring. *Woodruff* is a component of May Wine Cup. Experiment with other herbs such as *borage, lemon verbena, sorrel* and *tansy. Mustard* and *ginger* are both considered herbs by botanists, but are used in the manner of spices and are generally grouped with them. *Angelica's* candied stems are used in fruit cakes or as a decoration. *Filé* is a nonherb with herblike uses—made from the leaves of the sassafras tree. It is used to season Creole gumbos.

Menu

Family Reunion Buffet al Fresco

Fresh Coriander Dip, page 58
Carrot & Celery Sticks
Swedish Limpa, page 68
Cold British Boiled Beef, page 55
French Rolls & Basil Butter, page 112
Lettuce Leaves, Dill Pickles, Tomatoes
Sweet & Savory Mustard, page 152

Red-Hot Jelly, page 150,
Easy Fresh Relish, page 149
Dutch Potato Salad for a Crowd, page 27
Tropical-Fruit Salad
Citrus-Buttermilk Sherbet, page 71
Every-Which-Way Pound Cake, page 71
Oriental Lemonade, page 84
Iced Coffee

Crispy Herbed Potatoes

Rosemary gives unusual and delightful flavor to this simple side dish.

2 large baking potatoes, peeled
1/4 cup butter or margarine, melted

6 sprigs fresh rosemary, finely snipped
Salt and ground black pepper

Preheat oven to 350F (175C). Cut potatoes into 1/2-inch slices, then quarter the slices. Place in a single layer on a baking sheet. Brush with half the melted butter or margarine. Sprinkle with half the rosemary, then lightly with salt and pepper. Bake until golden, about 10 minutes. With a wide spatula, turn slices over. Brush with remaining butter or margarine, sprinkle with remaining rosemary, then lightly with salt and pepper. Bake until crisp and golden, about 10 minutes longer. Serve immediately. Makes 4 servings.

Spinach Salad Tangiers-Style

Fresh mint is the secret of this salad's wonderful flavor and aroma.

3 apples, cored, sliced
5 tablespoons lemon juice
1 lb. fresh spinach
1 medium cucumber, peeled, thinly sliced
3/4 cup thinly sliced celery
1/2 cup golden raisins
1/4 cup chopped walnuts

3/4 cup plain yogurt
1/2 teaspoon curry powder
2 tablespoons finely snipped fresh mint
1 garlic clove, minced
2 tablespoons finely chopped green onion
1/2 teaspoon salt
1/8 teaspoon ground black pepper

Place apple slices in a large bowl. Sprinkle with 3 tablespoons lemon juice; toss lightly to coat. Wash spinach well. Remove and discard tough stems. Dry spinach with paper towels. Tear spinach into bite-size pieces. Add to apples. Add cucumber, celery, raisins and walnuts. In a screwtop jar, combine yogurt, curry powder, mint, garlic, green onion, salt, pepper and remaining 2 tablespoons lemon juice. Cover tightly. Shake to combine well. Pour over spinach mixture just before serving. Toss lightly to coat. Makes 4 to 6 servings.

Tarragon Chicken Salad

Perfect for a summer lunch; serve with hot muffins and iced tea followed by lime sherbet.

1/2 cup vegetable oil
1/4 cup red-wine vinegar
2 tablespoons snipped fresh tarragon
1/4 teaspoon garlic powder
1/4 teaspoon salt
1/8 teaspoon red (cayenne) pepper

4 cups torn washed romaine leaves
4 cups torn washed fresh spinach leaves
1/2 lb. fresh mushrooms, thinly sliced
2 cups diced cooked chicken
1-1/2 cups diced Swiss cheese (6 oz.)
2 large ripe tomatoes, cut in wedges

In a screwtop jar, combine oil, vinegar, tarragon, garlic powder, salt and red pepper. Cover tightly. Shake to blend; set aside. In a shallow serving bowl, combine romaine and spinach leaves. Top with mushrooms, chicken and cheese. Toss lightly to combine. Shake dressing well and pour over salad. Toss again to coat well. Surround with tomato wedges. Serve immediately. Makes 6 main-course servings or 8 appetizer servings.

Hot Snap-Bean Salad   Photo on cover.

Summer savory and bacon season these colorful beans to dress up a simple meal.

1 lb. green beans, washed, ends removed
1 lb. wax beans, washed,
   ends and strings removed
4 bacon slices
1 tablespoon thinly sliced green onion
   with top
1/4 cup chopped red bell pepper
1/3 cup vegetable oil

1 tablespoon white vinegar
1 tablespoon lemon juice
1 tablespoon snipped fresh parsley
2 tablespoons snipped fresh summer savory
1 teaspoon sugar
1 teaspoon salt
1/8 teaspoon ground black pepper

In a large saucepan, cook green and wax beans in 1 inch of boiling salted water over high heat 10 minutes. Cover; reduce heat to medium. Cook until crisp-tender, about 5 minutes longer. Drain. While beans cook, in a medium skillet cook bacon until crisp. Drain on paper towels. Crumble bacon; set aside. Drain all but 2 tablespoons bacon fat from skillet. Add green onion and red pepper to skillet. Cook over medium heat until tender, about 5 minutes. Toss onion mixture with beans. In a small saucepan, heat oil, vinegar, lemon juice, parsley, savory and sugar to boiling. Stir in salt and pepper. Pour over beans. Toss to coat evenly. Spoon into a serving dish and sprinkle with crumbled bacon. Makes 6 servings.

Variations
Recipe may be prepared with all green or all wax beans.

Substitute 1-1/4 lbs. fresh peas, shelled, for the wax beans.

Ceci Salad Sicilian-Style

Garbanzo beans and salami with a medley of herbs make an excellent buffet-table dish.

2 (20-oz.) cans garbanzo beans, drained
1/4 lb. thinly sliced salami,
   cut in julienne strips
3 green onions, thinly sliced
1 (2-oz.) can chopped pimiento, drained
1 tablespoon finely snipped chives
1 tablespoon finely snipped fresh parsley
1/2 teaspoon garlic powder

1/4 teaspoon salt
4 teaspoons finely snipped fresh mint
1 teaspoon finely snipped fresh marjoram
1 teaspoon finely snipped fresh basil
1 teaspoon finely snipped fresh thyme
1/4 cup olive oil
1 tablespoon lemon juice
1 cup small cubes Provolone cheese (4 oz.)

Rinse garbanzo beans thoroughly with cold water; drain. Place in a large bowl. Add salami, green onions and pimiento. Toss to blend; set aside. In a screwtop jar, combine remaining ingredients except cheese. Cover tightly. Shake to blend. Pour over garbanzo-bean mixture; toss gently to combine. Cover; refrigerate, at least 3 hours. Before serving, toss again. Sprinkle with cheese. Makes 6 servings. Recipe may be doubled or tripled.

Variation
When fresh herbs are out of season, use fresh parsley and mint, which are usually available, along with frozen chives. For other herbs, substitute frozen or crumbled dried versions, about one third the amount of fresh herbs called for in the recipe.

Clockwise from top: Chervil Butter, page 111; Rosemary in Olive Oil, see box on page 31; Hot Snap-Bean Salad, page 24; Cheese & Basil Bubbles, page 26.

Greek-Style Lamb Pie

This delicious dill-seasoned meat-and-vegetable dish plus a salad makes a full meal.

3 lbs. boneless lamb shoulder
1-1/2 teaspoons salt
1/4 teaspoon ground black pepper
2 large carrots, scraped, sliced
2 large potatoes, peeled, sliced
1/3 cup thinly sliced celery
1 medium onion, chopped
Water

1 (11-oz.) pkg. pie-crust mix
2 teaspoons all-purpose flour
2 egg yolks
1/2 cup whipping cream
1 tablespoon lemon juice
2 teaspoons sugar
3/4 cup snipped fresh dill
1 (10-oz.) pkg. frozen peas, thawed

Trim excess fat from lamb. Cut meat into 1-inch cubes. Sprinkle with salt and pepper. In a 6-quart Dutch oven, combine lamb, carrots, potatoes, celery, onion and 2-1/2 cups water. Bring to a boil. Reduce heat. Cover and simmer, stirring occasionally, until lamb is tender, about 1 hour. While lamb cooks, prepare pie-crust mix as directed on package. On a lightly floured surface, roll out dough to a 12-inch circle. Cover with a dry cloth. Combine flour with 1 tablespoon water until smooth; set aside. In a medium bowl, beat egg yolks slightly. Beat in cream; set aside. Preheat oven to 350F (175C). Skim fat from lamb mixture. Drain liquid from lamb into a 2-cup measure. Add water to make 2 cups. Pour liquid into a medium saucepan; bring to a boil. Stir in flour mixture. Cook, stirring constantly, until bubbling and slightly thickened. Add lemon juice and sugar. Reduce heat to low. Into egg-yolk mixture, beat a small amount of hot sauce, then pour into remaining sauce. Heat gently, stirring; do not boil. Add drained lamb and vegetables. Stir in dill and peas. Spoon into a 3-quart casserole about 3 inches deep. Cut slits in pastry to let steam escape. Place over top of casserole; crimp edge. Bake until pastry is golden and pie is heated through, about 45 minutes. To reheat leftovers, remove and discard any remaining pastry. Stir 1/4 cup boiling water into lamb mixture. Cover and reheat about 45 minutes in preheated oven. Makes 10 servings.

Cheese & Basil Bubbles   Photo on cover and page 25.

Savory pull-apart quick bread is easy to make, and so good it disappears like magic.

2/3 cup grated Parmesan cheese (2 oz.)
2 tablespoons finely snipped
   fresh parsley
2 teaspoons finely snipped fresh basil
1/2 teaspoon garlic powder

1/2 teaspoon sweet paprika
3 cups biscuit baking mix
3/4 cup dairy sour cream
1/4 cup milk
1/4 cup butter or margarine, melted

Preheat oven to 400F (205C). Generously grease a 10-inch tube pan; set aside. In a pie plate or other flat dish, combine cheese, parsley, basil, garlic powder and paprika. Stir with a fork to blend; set aside. In a medium bowl, combine biscuit mix, sour cream and milk. Stir to blend, then beat vigorously 60 strokes. Turn out on a lightly floured surface. Gather into a ball and knead 10 times. Divide into 1-inch balls, rolling lightly between palms of both your hands to shape. Dip each ball into melted butter or margarine, then roll in cheese mixture to coat. Arrange balls about 1/4 inch apart in layers in prepared pan. If any cheese mixture remains, sprinkle over top. Bake in preheated oven until golden brown, about 20 minutes. Cool on a rack 5 minutes. Loosen from sides of pan and turn out. Makes about 8 servings.

Enchiladas Cilantro

Company coming? Serve this made-ahead Mexican dish, richly flavored with fresh coriander.

Salsa Roja con Cilantro, see below
4 cups shredded Monterey Jack cheese
  (1 lb.)
1/4 cup finely snipped fresh coriander
  (cilantro)
1-1/2 cups chopped sweet red onion

1 cup chopped pitted ripe olives
24 (6-inch) corn tortillas
1-1/2 cups coarsely crushed corn chips
4 hard-cooked eggs, chopped
4 green onions with tops, thinly sliced

Salsa Roja con Cilantro:
4 fresh jalapeño peppers, seeded, minced
5 large garlic cloves, minced
2 (28-oz.) cans whole plum tomatoes,
  undrained

1/4 cup finely snipped fresh coriander
  (cilantro)
1/4 cup corn oil
1 teaspoon salt

Prepare Salsa Roja con Cilantro. In a medium bowl, combine cheese and coriander. Put chopped onion and olives in separate small bowls. In an ungreased skillet over high heat, cook tortillas, one at a time, until softened, about 15 seconds on each side. Preheat oven to 350F (175C). Coat bottom and sides of a 3-quart shallow baking dish or two 1-1/2-quart shallow baking dishes with a thin film of oil; set aside. Place a heaping tablespoon of cheese mixture in center of each tortilla. Top with some chopped onion, then some chopped olives. Roll up and place, seam-side down, in prepared dishes. Dish can be made in advance. Cover and refrigerate filled tortillas in baking dishes, and sauce in separate container. Before baking, spoon Salsa Roja con Cilantro over tortillas. Bake in preheated oven, 25 minutes if dish was at room temperature, 50 minutes if it was refrigerated. Combine corn chips, eggs and sliced green onions; sprinkle over top of casserole. Return to oven for 3 minutes. Makes 12 servings.

Salsa Roja con Cilantro:
In a large saucepan, combine peppers and garlic. Chop tomatoes coarsely. Add to saucepan with juice. Add coriander, oil and salt. Bring to a boil. Reduce heat. Simmer, uncovered, stirring frequently, 25 minutes. Makes about 6 cups.

Dutch Potato Salad for a Crowd

Fresh dill and red onions give new dimensions to an old summertime favorite.

2-1/2 cups Lancaster County Dressing,
  page 53, made with
  3 tablespoons sugar
2/3 cup finely snipped fresh dill
5 lbs. new potatoes, cooked, peeled, diced

2/3 cup finely chopped sweet red onion
8 hard-cooked eggs, shelled
Salt and ground black pepper to taste
Fresh dill sprigs, if desired

Prepare Lancaster County Dressing; pour into a large bowl. Stir in dill. Add potatoes and onion; toss lightly to coat well. Cut eggs in half crosswise, then cut each half into quarters. Add to potato mixture and toss again. Season to taste with salt and pepper. Cover; refrigerate until ready to serve. Flavor increases with standing. Garnish with dill sprigs, if desired. Makes 12 servings.

Green Feather Pinwheels

Fresh oregano supplies color and flavor, onion adds zest to these yeast rolls.

1 (1/4-oz.) pkg. active dry yeast
  (1 tablespoon)
1/4 cup warm water (110F, 45C)
3 tablespoons butter or margarine
1 cup milk
1 tablespoon sugar

1 teaspoon salt
3-1/2 cups all-purpose or bread flour
1 medium onion, finely chopped
2 tablespoons finely snipped fresh oregano
Celery salt

In a large bowl, sprinkle yeast over warm water. Let stand until bubbly, about 10 minutes. In a small saucepan, heat 1 tablespoon butter or margarine with milk until softened and partially melted. Cool to lukewarm. Stir milk mixture, sugar and salt into yeast mixture. Add 2 cups flour; beat to mix. Add 1 cup flour and beat until blended. Turn out onto a lightly floured surface. Clean and generously grease bowl; set aside. Knead in remaining 1/2 cup flour until dough is smooth and elastic, about 10 minutes. Place dough in greased bowl, turning to grease all sides. Cover with a dry cloth. Let rise in a warm place, free from drafts, until doubled in bulk, about 1-1/2 hours. While dough rises, heat remaining 2 tablespoons butter or margarine in a small skillet. Add onion; sauté until soft but not brown. Generously grease a round 10-inch pan. When dough has risen, punch down and knead several times. On a lightly floured surface, roll out dough to a 16" x 11" rectangle. Sprinkle dough evenly with onion, reserving cooking butter or margarine. Sprinkle dough with oregano, then lightly with celery salt. Roll up, jelly-roll-fashion, from long side. Cut dough into 1-inch slices. Arrange slices, cut-side up, in prepared pan so they just touch. Brush with butter or margarine in which onion was cooked. Let rise until doubled in bulk, 30 to 45 minutes. Preheat oven to 375F (190C). Bake rolls until golden brown, about 30 minutes. Remove from pan. Cool on a rack 10 minutes. Serve warm. Makes 16 rolls.

Giant Dilly Popovers

Serve these with corned-beef hash and poached eggs for a perfect Sunday brunch.

1 cup all-purpose flour
1/4 teaspoon salt
2 eggs

1 cup milk
1 tablespoon finely snipped fresh dill
1 tablespoon melted butter or margarine

Place all ingredients in blender or food processor. Process at medium speed 1 minute in blender, or 10 to 15 seconds in food processor. Let stand, covered, at room temperature 30 minutes. Batter may be prepared and refrigerated up to 24 hours in advance. Preheat oven to 400F (205C). Generously grease six 6-ounce glass custard cups. Place on a baking sheet. Process batter in blender or food processor at medium speed 20 seconds. Divide among prepared custard cups. Bake in preheated oven until puffed and golden brown, 35 to 40 minutes. Do not open oven door during first 20 minutes of baking. Serve immediately. Makes 6 servings.

Variation
Batter can be baked in 10 well-buttered muffin tins.

How to Make Green Feather Pinwheels

1/Roll out dough. Sprinkle with onion, oregano and celery salt. Roll up dough from long side.

2/Cut into 1-inch slices. Arrange slices in pan, cut-side up, barely touching.

Rosy Buttered Onions

Serve with liver, steak or London broil.

6 large red Italian onions, peeled
1 tablespoon snipped fresh rosemary leaves
   or 1 teaspoon dried leaf rosemary,
   crumbled

1/4 cup butter or margarine,
   room temperature
1 teaspoon salt
1/4 teaspoon ground black pepper

Cut onions in half vertically, then cut halves into 1/8-inch slices. Place onion slices in a large skillet. Add cold water until about 1 inch deep. Bring to a boil over high heat. Cover skillet and continue cooking over high heat 5 minutes. Uncover; reduce heat to medium. Cook 5 minutes longer. Drain off water. Reduce heat to low. Add rosemary. Cut butter or margarine into pieces. Add 1 piece at a time tossing onion slices with a fork so they are coated with melted butter or margarine. Sprinkle with salt and pepper; toss again. Serve immediately. Makes 4 servings.

Three-B Vegetable Soup

Bay leaf, basil and beans—the chief flavors in this hearty dish.

1/2 lb. dried white kidney beans
6 cups water
3 medium zucchini, diced
3 medium, white turnips, peeled, diced
1 large potato, peeled, diced
6 medium carrots, scraped, thinly sliced
2 celery stalks with leaves, thinly sliced
2 sweet red onions, coarsely chopped

1 small yellow onion, peeled
4 whole cloves
1 bay leaf
1 (17-oz.) can whole plum tomatoes,
  undrained
5 tablespoons snipped fresh basil
1-1/2 tablespoons salt
4 drops hot-pepper sauce

One day before serving, soak beans overnight in cold water to cover, even if package says soaking is not necessary. Drain beans; rinse in cold water. Place in a large pot. Add 6 cups water; bring to a boil. Add zucchini, turnips, potato, carrots, celery and red onions. Stud yellow onion with cloves; add to pot. Add bay leaf, tomatoes with liquid, 3 tablespoons basil, salt and pepper sauce. Reduce heat to low. Simmer, covered, until beans are tender, about 2-1/2 hours. Remove bay leaf and yellow onion. Serve immediately. Or, refrigerate overnight to develop richer flavor; reheat to serve. Sprinkle with remaining 2 tablespoons basil. Makes 4-1/2 quarts, or 10 to 14 main-dish servings.

Herbed Leek & Spinach Soup

Beautiful, savory pale-green soup to serve topped with homemade croutons.

1/4 cup butter or margarine
4 medium leeks, cleaned, sliced
1 medium onion, chopped
2 celery stalks, thinly sliced
6 cups Chicken Stock, page 98,
  or canned chicken broth
1 bay leaf
1-1/2 teaspoons salt

2 tablespoons snipped fresh parsley
1-1/2 tablespoons snipped fresh thyme
1/4 teaspoon ground white pepper
1 lb. fresh spinach, washed, drained
1 cup half and half
4 thin slices white bread, crusts trimmed,
  cut in 1/2-inch squares

In a medium skillet, melt butter or margarine over low heat. Add leeks, onion and celery. Cook, stirring, 10 minutes. With a slotted spoon, transfer vegetables to a 5- or 6-quart Dutch oven or large saucepan; reserve butter or margarine in skillet. To Dutch oven or saucepan, add stock or broth, bay leaf, salt, 1 tablespoon parsley, thyme and pepper. Remove heavy stems from spinach. Add spinach leaves to Dutch oven or saucepan. Bring mixture to a boil. Reduce heat; cover and simmer 20 minutes. Remove bay leaf. In blender, puree mixture in 3 batches, 15 seconds each on high speed. Return to Dutch oven or saucepan. Stir in half and half. Place over very low heat until hot; do not boil. While soup heats, place skillet with reserved butter or margarine over medium heat. Add bread squares. Sauté until lightly browned. Add remaining 1 tablespoon parsley to croutons; toss lightly to blend. Spoon soup into individual dishes. Top with croutons. Makes 6 to 8 servings.

Variation
To serve soup chilled, reduce butter or margarine to 2 tablespoons; omit bread. After stirring in half and half, refrigerate soup, covered, until icy cold. Just before serving, stir well and sprinkle with remaining 1 tablespoon parsley.

A Loaf To Remember

Homemade bread, fragrant with fresh rosemary, is an unforgettable treat.

1 (1/4-oz.) pkg. active dry yeast
  (1 tablespoon)
2 tablespoons finely snipped fresh
  rosemary
1 cup warm water (110F, 45C)
1/2 teaspoon sugar

1 teaspoon salt
1 cup whole-wheat flour
About 2-1/2 cups all-purpose or
  bread flour
1/4 cup butter or margarine, melted

In a large bowl, sprinkle yeast and 1 tablespoon rosemary over warm water. Let stand until bubbly, about 10 minutes. Stir in sugar, salt, whole-wheat flour and 3/4 cup all-purpose or bread flour. With a wooden spoon or heavy-duty mixer, beat until dough pulls away from the bowl in stretchy ribbons. Gradually beat in 1-1/4 cups all-purpose or bread flour to make a stiff dough. Turn out onto a lightly floured surface. Clean and grease bowl; set aside. Knead dough until smooth and elastic, about 10 minutes, adding more all-purpose flour if required. Place dough in greased bowl, turning to coat all sides. Cover with a dry cloth. Let rise in a warm place, free from drafts, until doubled in bulk, about 1 hour. Punch down dough. Turn out onto lightly floured surface. Knead lightly 10 strokes. Grease an 8" x 4" loaf pan. Shape dough into a smooth loaf. Place in pan. Brush top lightly with melted butter or margarine; reserve remaining butter or margarine. Let loaf rise until doubled in bulk, about 1 hour. Preheat oven to 375F (190C). Brush top of loaf again with butter or margarine and sprinkle with remaining 1 tablespoon rosemary leaves. Bake until golden brown and loaf sounds hollow when tapped, about 45 minutes. Turn out of pan. Cool completely on a rack. Makes 1 loaf.

How To Preserve Fresh Herbs

To store fresh herbs up to one week in your refrigerator, wash gently in cool water; shake off excess water. Gather the herbs into a bunch and place, like a bouquet, in a small container of water. Then place a small plastic bag over all. Secure airtight and refrigerate.

If you have a summer garden, you can preserve your own herbs for out-of-season use. **To freeze herbs,** strip away heavy stems. Wash the herbs carefully; drain and dry on paper towels. Freeze whole sprigs in plastic bags, or snip and pack in containers from which you can remove as much as you need at one time. **Dry herbs** slowly but thoroughly in the sun, in the oven, or in a microwave oven, where they dry particularly well. Follow directions that come with your microwave. Then package in paper bags, or store in clean, dry small bottles in a dark place. Herbs such as tarragon and dill may be preserved—almost as good as fresh—**in distilled white vinegar.** Store them in the refrigerator. When you want some, pull out a sprig or two, rinse lightly and pat dry. Or keep herbs often used in oil-based dishes, such as basil and oregano, **in olive oil.** Store at cool room temperature.

How to Make Tarragon-Stuffed Red Snapper

1/Spoon stuffing into fish cavity.

2/Close opening with picks or skewers.

Crusty Chicken

Serve hot for one meal, cold for another—equally delicious either way.

2 (about 2-1/2-lb.) broiler-fryer chickens,
  cut up
1 cup butter or margarine
3/4 cup Dijon-style mustard
1 teaspoon snipped fresh tarragon

2 cups fresh breadcrumbs
1/2 cup grated Parmesan cheese (1-1/2 oz.)
3 tablespoons snipped fresh parsley
1/8 teaspoon red (cayenne) pepper

Preheat oven to 350F (175C). Pat chicken dry. Place in a 13'' x 9'' baking pan. In a small sauce-pan, combine butter or margarine, mustard and tarragon. Stir over low heat until butter or margarine melts. On a sheet of waxed paper or foil, combine breadcrumbs, cheese, parsley and red pepper. With a fork, stir to blend. Spoon mustard mixture evenly over chicken, turning pieces to coat on all sides. One at a time, dip chicken pieces in crumb mixture, turning and patting with your fingers to coat evenly. Return each piece to its place in the pan before coating another piece. Bake in preheated oven 30 minutes. Turn chicken pieces. Bake 15 to 20 minutes longer or until chicken is crisp and golden brown. Makes 8 servings.

Tarragon-Stuffed Red Snapper

Fish and tarragon make a happy combination in this handsome, flavorful dish.

1 whole (2-1/2- to 3-lb.) red snapper
1/3 cup butter or margarine
1 tablespoon lemon juice
1/2 cup thinly sliced green onion
2 tablespoons snipped fresh tarragon

1/2 teaspoon salt
1/8 teaspoon ground white pepper
2 cups fresh breadcrumbs
1 lemon, cut in 6 to 8 wedges
Fresh parsley sprigs

Wash fish inside and out under cold running water. Drain well; pat dry with paper towels. Preheat oven to 400F (205C). Line a 13" x 9" baking pan with foil; grease foil. In a medium skillet, melt butter or margarine. Add 2 tablespoons melted butter or margarine to lemon juice; set aside. In skillet, cook green onion over medium-low heat until soft but not browned, about 3 minutes. Stir in tarragon, salt and pepper. Add breadcrumbs; toss to combine. Spoon stuffing into fish cavity. Close opening with wooden picks or skewers. Pour reserved lemon-juice mixture over fish. Bake in preheated oven until fish flakes easily when pierced with a fork, 35 to 40 minutes. With a large spatula, transfer stuffed fish to a heated platter. Surround with lemon wedges and parsley sprigs. Makes 6 to 8 servings.

Variations
Whole striped bass can be substituted for the red snapper. If fresh tarragon is not available, use 1 teaspoon dried leaf tarragon mixed with 2 tablespoons snipped fresh parsley.

Vermicelli with Fresh Sage

This all-fresh pasta sauce has a mouth-watering aroma as it cooks.

60 fresh sage leaves
1/2 cup olive oil
2 medium carrots, scraped,
   finely chopped
2 garlic cloves, minced
1/2 cup finely chopped onion
4 lbs. fresh plum tomatoes,
   coarsely chopped

1/4 teaspoon sugar
1 teaspoon salt
1/4 teaspoon coarsely
   ground black pepper
5 qts. water
2 tablespoons vegetable oil
1 tablespoon salt
1 lb. vermicelli noodles

On a flat surface, set out three 3-inch squares single-thickness cheesecloth. Place 20 sage leaves in center of each square. Tie firmly with cotton string; set aside. In a large, heavy saucepan over medium heat, combine olive oil, carrots, garlic and onion. Cook until soft but not browned, about 6 minutes. Add tomatoes and sage bundles. Reduce heat. Cover and simmer 25 minutes, stirring frequently. Stir in sugar and 1 teaspoon salt. Remove and discard sage bundles from sauce. Stir in pepper. Keep sauce warm over lowest heat. In a 6-quart pot, bring 5 quarts water to boil with vegetable oil and 1 tablespoon salt. Add vermicelli to boiling water. Boil briskly until tender but firm to the bite, 6 or 7 minutes. Drain well. Add vermicelli to sauce and toss over low heat until well coated. Makes 6 servings.

Seeds, Buds & Berries

The familiar, tangy flavor of many plants lies in their seeds. But more often than not we use a part or extract of the seed rather than the seed itself. We can buy *anise,* a seed of an herb of the parsley family, ground or as an extract. We consider the ground form of *cardamom, cumin* and *mustard* as spices because that is how we are accustomed to using them. But it is whole, untreated seeds with which we are concerned here. The most frequently used in our cooking are: *anise, caraway, celery, dill, fennel, poppy* and *sesame.* Anise, caraway and fennel seeds have a similar licorice flavor. The celery seed we buy is not the seed of the familiar plant, but that of a kind of wild celery called *smallage,* that grows in Mediterranean regions.

A berry such as *allspice* can be purchased whole and ground or grated at home. Grinding releases flavor and aroma far greater than in the ready-ground form. On the other hand, *juniper* is available only as whole, dried berries. Its primary use is in the distilling of gin. The flavorful berry can enliven your favorite meat sauce.

The most familiar bud in our kitchens is the *caper.* It is purchased pickled in vinegar with a little salt, and adds piquant flavor to seafood, salads and sauces. Capers range in size from small to the large Italian-type.

Let's not forget the plump green seed of the familiar garden *nasturtium.* It is seldom available commercially, but it is easy to pickle at home. It provides a delicious and unusual flavoring. Its zesty, peppery taste makes it welcome in any dish that calls for capers.

Chinese *cassia buds* are usually available in specialty food shops or by mail. They are somewhat sweet, have a flavor that combines cinnamon and cloves, and are most often used in confections.

If you are not familiar with these small wonders of the flavoring world, this section will point the way to some of the many uses to which they can be put in your kitchen.

Menu

Company-Coming Dinner : Winter

Kir
French-Fried Walnuts, page 154
Chinese Tea Eggs, page 78
Lemony Coriander Soup, page 38
Roast Veal San Francisco-Style, page 92
A Loaf to Remember, page 31
Mint-Sprinkled Baby Carrots
Tossed Green Salad
California Poppy-Seed Cake, page 45
Pinot Chardonnay Wine
After-Dinner Coffee

Pickled Nasturtium Seeds

Preserve the seeds in late summer—they will keep a year or more.

2 cups nasturtium seeds
Distilled white vinegar

Pick nasturtium seeds when they have just set and are freshly green. Seeds are large and easy to gather. Place in a small glass or ceramic bowl. Add vinegar to cover. Let stand at room temperature 48 hours. Wash 2 to 4 small canning jars in hot soapy water; rinse. Keep hot until needed. Prepare lids as manufacturer directs. Drain nasturtium seeds; place in a small saucepan. Add fresh vinegar to cover. Bring to a boil. Reduce heat. Cook at a slow boil 10 minutes. Fill and close 1 jar at a time. Spoon hot mixture to within 1/4 inch of jar rim, spooning seeds and vinegar evenly into jar. Release trapped air. Wipe rim of jar. Attach lid. Place filled jar in hot water in water-bath canner. Fill and close remaining jars. Cover all jars with hot water. Bring to a boil. Boil 15 minutes at sea level; add 1 minute for each 1000 feet of altitude. Remove jars from canner; do not tighten lids. Cool on a rack on towels in a place free from drafts. Press down on center of lid. If lid is down, seal is completed. If lid goes down as you press, remove ring and tip jar to side to see if there is leakage. Holding edge of lid with several fingers of 1 hand, lift jar 1 inch above table. If lid holds, seal is completed. Refrigerate jars that are not sealed. Label and store sealed jars in a cool, dark place up to 2 years. Refrigerate up to 3 months after opening. Makes about 2-1/2 cups.

Moroccan Panned Vegetables

Use the crunchy topping on other vegetables, too, or sprinkle on heated buttered crackers.

1/2 cup Moroccan Topper, see below
1 tablespoon olive oil
2 tablespoons butter or margarine
1 small onion, sliced
1 small eggplant, peeled, sliced,
   slices quartered

2 medium zucchini, sliced
2 medium, yellow crookneck squash, sliced
10 cherry tomatoes, halved

Moroccan Topper:
1 cup pine nuts
1 cup sesame seeds
1/4 cup coriander seeds
2 tablespoons dried leaf mint

1 teaspoon salt
1/2 teaspoon turmeric
1/4 teaspoon red (cayenne) pepper

Prepare Moroccan Topper. In a large skillet, heat oil and butter or margarine. Add onion. Cook over medium heat until soft but not browned, about 3 minutes. Add eggplant. Reduce heat to low. Cook, covered, 3 minutes. Add zucchini and crookneck squash. Cook, covered, 5 minutes, adding more butter or margarine and oil if necessary. Stir in tomatoes. Cook, uncovered, 3 minutes. Turn into a hot serving dish. Sprinkle with 1/2 cup Moroccan Topper. Makes 6 servings.

Moroccan Topper:
Preheat oven to 350F (175C). Spread pine nuts on an ungreased baking sheet. Bake until golden, 10 to 15 minutes, shaking pan often. Spoon into blender; let stand at room temperature. Spread sesame seeds on same baking sheet. Bake until golden, about 5 minutes, stirring often. Pour into blender; let stand 10 minutes. Add remaining ingredients. At medium speed, turn blender on and off several times until mixture is coarsely ground. Pour into a screwtop jar. Cover tightly and store in a cool dry place. Makes about 2 cups.

Old-Country Breadsticks   Photo on page 87.

Crisp, golden brown, fennel-flavored—just right with salad or pasta.

1 (1/4-oz.) pkg. active dry yeast (1 tablespoon)	1-1/2 teaspoons salt
	1 tablespoon fennel seeds
3/4 cup warm water (110F, 45C)	4-1/2 cups all-purpose flour
3/4 cup vegetable oil	1 egg
3/4 cup beer	1 tablespoon cold water

In a large bowl, sprinkle yeast over warm water. Let stand until bubbly, about 10 minutes. Add oil, beer, salt and fennel seeds. Beat in 3-1/2 cups flour, making a soft dough. On a dry surface, spread remaining 1 cup flour. Turn dough out onto flour. Clean and grease bowl; set aside. Knead dough to incorporate flour until dough is smooth and elastic. Place dough in bowl, turning to grease all sides. Cover with a dry cloth. Let rise in a warm place, free from drafts, until doubled in bulk, about 1 hour. Place wire racks on each of 2 large baking sheets. In a small bowl, beat egg and cold water; set aside. Punch down dough. Knead 5 or 6 times to release air bubbles. Preheat oven to 350F (175C). Pinch off 3/4-inch balls of dough. Roll each piece between your hands or on work surface to make an 9-inch rope. Cut ropes in half crosswise. Place ropes across racks, about 1/2 inch apart. Brush gently with egg-water mixture. Bake in preheated oven until evenly golden brown, about 35 minutes. Place on other racks or on foil to cool. Wrap airtight in foil. Store at room temperature. Makes about 50 breadsticks.

Dill-Seed Cottage Loaf

A moist, easy batter bread, speckled with crunchy, flavorful dill seeds.

1 (1/4-oz.) pkg. active dry yeast (1 tablespoon)	1/2 cup plain yogurt
	1 tablespoon minced onion
1/4 cup warm water (110F, 45C)	1/4 teaspoon baking soda
1 tablespoon honey	2 tablespoons dill seeds
1 tablespoon vegetable oil	1 cup whole-wheat flour
1 teaspoon salt	1 cup all-purpose flour,
1 egg, slightly beaten	preferably unbleached
1/2 cup small-curd cottage cheese	

In a large bowl, sprinkle yeast over water. Let stand until bubbly, about 10 minutes. Add honey, oil, salt, egg, cottage cheese, yogurt, onion, baking soda and dill seeds. Mix well. Add whole-wheat flour. Stir until flour is moistened. Add all-purpose flour. Stir to moisten. Beat 2 minutes. Cover with a dry cloth or plastic wrap. Let rise in a warm place, free from drafts, until doubled in bulk, at least 2 hours. Preheat oven to 350F (175C). Butter a 2-quart round or oval ovenproof bowl or casserole. Punch down dough. Place in prepared bowl. Bake until golden brown, about 30 minutes. Turn out onto a rack to cool. Makes 1 loaf.

How to Make Old-Country Breadsticks

1/Pinch off 3/4-inch balls of dough. Roll each between your hands into a 9-inch rope.

2/Arrange ropes across wire racks on baking sheets. Brush with egg-water mixture.

Farm-Style Sausage Patties

Serve these smoky treats with Old-Fashioned Buckwheat Cakes, page 68, for a hearty brunch.

2 lbs. ground pork
1 medium onion, finely chopped
1 garlic clove, minced
1 teaspoon salt
1 teaspoon chili powder

1/2 teaspoon fennel seeds
1/4 teaspoon smoke-flavor extract
1/8 teaspoon red (cayenne) pepper
1/8 teaspoon ground allspice
2 eggs, slightly beaten

In a large bowl, combine pork, onion and garlic. With your hands or a spoon, mix well. Sprinkle with salt, chili powder, fennel seeds, smoke extract, red pepper and allspice. Mix again to blend. Mix in eggs until blended. Shape into 3-inch patties. Arrange patties in a cold, large skillet. Cook over low heat until fat begins to run from patties. Increase heat to medium-high. Cook until browned and no longer pink inside, 3 to 4 minutes on each side. Drain on paper towels. Serve immediately. Makes 8 servings.

Peking-Style Beef Ribs

Anise seeds give this hearty dish an excellent and unusual flavor.

2-1/2 lbs. beef short ribs
12 anise seeds
2 tablespoons soy sauce
1/2 cup dry red wine
1 garlic clove, minced
1/8 teaspoon ground ginger

Herb Bag, see below
1-1/2 cups Beef Stock, page 98,
   or canned beef broth
1 tablespoon cornstarch
1 tablespoon cold water

Herb Bag:
1 garlic clove, peeled
1 tablespoon dried parsley flakes
1 teaspoon dried leaf basil
1 teaspoon dried leaf rosemary

1 teaspoon dried leaf oregano
2 bay leaves
6 black peppercorns

Cut short ribs into 1-inch pieces. Remove excess fat. Place ribs in a deep glass or ceramic bowl. In a mortar or small bowl, crush anise seeds with pestle or back of a heavy spoon until fine. Combine crushed anise seeds, soy sauce, wine, garlic and ginger; stir to blend. Pour over ribs. Let stand at room temperature 2 hours or refrigerate overnight, turning ribs occasionally so all parts come in contact with marinade. Remove ribs, reserving marinade. Place ribs, fat side down, in a heavy skillet. Cook over medium-low heat, turning to brown all sides. Drain off fat from ribs. Prepare Herb Bag. Combine reserved marinade with stock or broth. Pour over ribs. Add Herb Bag. Bring to a boil. Cover tightly and reduce heat. Simmer until ribs are tender, 2 to 2-1/2 hours. Discard Herb Bag. Arrange cooked ribs in a serving dish. Stir cornstarch into cold water until smooth. Add to simmering liquid in skillet, stirring constantly until thickened. Pour over ribs. Serve immediately. Makes 4 servings.

Herb Bag:
On a 3-inch square of double-thickness cheesecloth, combine all ingredients. Bring edges of square together to form a bag. Tie with kitchen string.

Lemony Coriander Soup

With chicken stock in the freezer, this elegant soup is a quick and easy dish.

2 qts. Chicken Stock, page 98,
   or canned chicken broth
1 large carrot, halved lengthwise
1 medium onion, halved
10 fresh parsley sprigs
10 coriander seeds

3 tablespoons finely snipped fresh
   coriander (cilantro)
4 teaspoons lemon juice
Salt and ground white pepper to taste
6 slices Melba toast
Butter or margarine

In a large saucepan, combine stock or broth, carrot, onion, parsley and coriander seeds. Bring to a boil. Reduce heat. Simmer, covered, 25 minutes. Strain into a second large saucepan. Add 2 tablespoons snipped coriander leaves and lemon juice. Season to taste with salt and white pepper. Simmer 5 minutes to heat through. While soup heats, spread Melba toast lightly with butter or margarine. Sprinkle with remaining 1 tablespoon coriander leaves. Ladle soup into individual serving bowls. Float a slice of Melba toast on each. Serve immediately. Makes 6 servings.

Cutlets Piccata

Turkey is substituted for high-priced veal in this easy Italian-style dish.

1/2 cup all-purpose flour
1/2 teaspoon dried leaf oregano,
   crumbled
1/2 teaspoon salt
1/4 teaspoon ground white pepper
8 turkey-breast cutlets,
   1/4 to 1/2 inch thick

2 tablespoons butter or margarine
1 tablespoon vegetable oil
1/4 cup lemon juice
3 tablespoons well-drained capers

In a pie plate, combine flour, oregano, salt and pepper; stir to blend. Dredge cutlets in flour mixture. With a meat mallet or edge of a heavy saucer, pound cutlets on both sides to flatten them slightly. In a large skillet, heat butter or margarine with oil over low heat. Add cutlets. Cook, covered, 5 minutes. Remove cover and increase heat to medium. Continue to cook cutlets until lightly browned, opaque and firm, 3 to 4 minutes more on each side. Arrange cooked cutlets on a warm platter; keep warm. Drain off all but 2 teaspoons fat from skillet. Add lemon juice. Cook 1 minute over high heat, stirring and scraping pan with a wooden spoon. Stir in capers. Pour over cutlets. Serve immediately. Makes 4 servings.

Turkish-Style Lentil Soup

Richly flavored with sausage and fennel—just right on a blustery winter day.

1 lb. lentils
3 qts. water
2 tablespoons beef-flavor
   instant bouillon powder or granules
1-1/2 teaspoons fennel seeds
1 lb. sweet Italian sausage
1 (28-oz.) can whole plum tomatoes,
   undrained
2 medium onions, chopped

3/4 cup chopped celery
3/4 cup chopped carrots
3 tablespoons snipped fresh coriander
   (cilantro) or fresh parsley
1 bay leaf
1-1/2 teaspoons salt
1/4 teaspoon ground black pepper
1 tablespoon lemon juice

In a 6-quart Dutch oven or saucepan, combine lentils, water, bouillon powder or granules and 1 teaspoon fennel seeds. Bring to a boil. Boil 2 minutes. Remove from heat. Cover and let stand 1 hour. Bring to a boil again; reduce heat. Simmer, covered, until lentils are tender, about 45 minutes. While lentils cook, remove and discard casings from sausage. In a large skillet, cook sausage over medium heat until browned, stirring frequently to break up sausage. Drain off fat. Add remaining 1/2 teaspoon fennel seeds. Drain tomato liquid into sausage mixture. Chop tomatoes coarsely. Add to sausage mixture. Stir in remaining ingredients except lentil mixture. Bring to a boil; reduce heat. Simmer, covered, until vegetables are tender, 30 to 40 minutes. Discard bay leaf. Pour lentil mixture into blender, about 4 cups at a time, or into food processor, about 2 cups at a time. Process at high speed until smooth. Pour pureed lentil mixture into Dutch oven or saucepan. Stir in sausage mixture. Cook over low heat 15 minutes, stirring occasionally. Makes 8 main-dish servings.

Swedish Stuffed-Egg Salad

With a cup of soup and crusty bread, this makes a light supper for a hot summer night.

9 hard-cooked eggs, shelled
2 tablespoons mayonnaise
1/4 teaspoon prepared yellow mustard
1/8 teaspoon red (cayenne) pepper
3 tablespoons drained capers
1 medium cucumber

1/2 fresh pineapple
Lemon-Pepper Vinaigrette, see below
1 head Boston or butter lettuce
6 large slices smoked salmon
3 tomatoes, cut in wedges
Fresh watercress sprigs, if desired

Lemon-Pepper Vinaigrette:
1/4 teaspoon salt
1/4 teaspoon coarsely ground black pepper
1/4 teaspoon onion juice

2 tablespoons lemon juice
1/2 cup vegetable oil
2 teaspoons finely snipped fresh parsley

Halve eggs lengthwise. Place whites on a plate, yolks in a small bowl. To yolks, add mayonnaise, mustard and red pepper. Blend well, mashing yolks until smooth. Mince 1 tablespoon capers and stir into yolk mixture. Fill whites with yolk mixture. Cover and refrigerate. With a fork, score peel of cucumber end to end. Cut cucumber in thin slices; set aside. Peel and core pineapple. Cut into fingers. Prepare Lemon-Pepper Vinaigrette. Line 6 individual serving plates with lettuce leaves and cucumber slices. Place 3 egg halves in center of each plate, small ends in and touching. Cut each salmon slice in quarters and place between eggs. Surround with tomato and pineapple slices. Sprinkle salmon with remaining 2 tablespoons capers. Garnish with watercress sprigs, if desired. Pass Lemon-Pepper Vinaigrette separately. Makes 6 servings.

Lemon-Pepper Vinaigrette:
In a small screwtop jar, combine salt, pepper, onion juice and lemon juice. Shake to combine. Add oil and parsley. Cover and shake again to blend. Refrigerate until serving time. Before serving, shake well and pour into a cruet. Makes about 2/3 cup.

Honeyed Sesame Spread

So great on bread or toast, it will give peanut butter a run for its money.

1 cup sesame seeds
2 tablespoons honey

1/4 cup boiling water
1/4 teaspoon salt

In a heavy skillet, shake and stir sesame seeds over medium-low heat until lightly browned. Let cool about 5 minutes. In blender or nut grinder, grind sesame seeds as fine as possible. In a small bowl or screwtop jar, combine ground sesame seeds, honey, water and salt. Cover and refrigerate. Recipe may be doubled. Makes about 1 cup before doubling.

Variation
Spiced Sesame Butter: Add 1/4 teaspoon ground cinnamon and 1/8 teaspoon ground allspice to sesame spread. Stir into 1/2 cup soft butter or margarine. Serve with pancakes or waffles.

Swedish Stuffed-Egg Salad, Swedish Limpa, page 68, Danish Dill Butter, page 116

Turkey Salad Oriental-Style

Where there is turkey, there are leftovers. Here's a fine way to deal with them.

Sesame-Seed Dressing, see below
1 (10-oz.) pkg. frozen snow peas, thawed
1/2 lb. fresh bean sprouts

2-1/2 cups diced cooked turkey
1/4 cup thinly sliced green onions

Sesame-Seed Dressing:
1/2 cup sesame seeds
1/2 cup vegetable oil
3 garlic cloves, minced
3 tablespoons lemon juice

1-1/2 tablespoons soy sauce
1-1/2 tablespoons white-wine vinegar
2 teaspoons minced gingerroot or
   1/2 teaspoon ground ginger

Prepare Sesame-Seed Dressing. Cover and refrigerate. Place snow peas in a strainer or sieve. Set in a pan of boiling water. Remove from heat and let stand 2 minutes. Drain well. In a serving bowl, combine snow peas, bean sprouts and turkey. Add 1/4 cup Sesame-Seed Dressing. Toss gently with 2 forks. Sprinkle with green onions. Makes 4 servings.

Sesame-Seed Dressing:
In a large skillet, shake and stir sesame seeds over medium heat until golden brown. Turn into a small bowl. Let stand at room temperature until cool. Add remaining ingredients. Stir to blend. Stir again just before using. Makes about 1-1/4 cups.

Circassian Cauliflower

Roasted seeds blend their flavors into an exotic seasoning for this salad.

2 medium heads cauliflower,
   broken into flowerets
2 teaspoons sesame seeds
1 teaspoon mustard seeds
1/2 teaspoon cumin seeds
1/4 teaspoon coriander seeds
8 whole cardamom pods

1/2 cup butter or margarine
5 medium onions, thinly sliced
2 teaspoons caraway seeds
2 cups plain yogurt
Salt and ground black pepper to taste
1 bunch fresh coriander (cilantro)

Cook cauliflower in a large saucepan of boiling salted water until crisp-tender. Rinse well with cold water to stop cooking. Drain well. Place in a medium bowl; set aside. In a small skillet, combine sesame, mustard, cumin and coriander seeds. Break cardamom pods and add seeds to skillet; discard pods. Place skillet over medium heat. Shake and stir seeds until mustard seeds begin to pop open. Remove from heat. In blender, or with mortar and pestle, grind roasted seeds; set aside. In a medium skillet, melt butter or margarine. Add onions. Cook over medium-low heat, stirring frequently, until soft, about 10 minutes. Increase heat to high. Continue to cook and stir until onions just begin to brown. Add caraway seeds and ground seeds. Stirring constantly, cook 1 minute. Spoon onion mixture over cauliflower. Stir yogurt until smooth. Pour over cauliflower. Toss gently to mix. Season to taste with salt and pepper. Cover and refrigerate overnight. Before serving, bring to room temperature. Line a large serving plate with fresh coriander. Mound cauliflower mixture over coriander. Makes 8 servings.

Garlic-Herb Bread

Halve slices to serve as an appetizer, or leave whole to accompany any pasta dish.

2 teaspoons Garlic-Herb Seasoning,
  see below
1 loaf crusty French bread

1 cup butter or margarine,
  room temperature
1/4 cup sesame seeds

Garlic-Herb Seasoning:
2 tablespoons dried leaf marjoram
2 tablespoons dried leaf oregano
2 tablespoons dried leaf rosemary
2 tablespoons dried leaf basil
2 tablespoons dried parsley flakes

1 tablespoon onion powder
1 tablespoon dried leaf thyme
1 tablespoon salt
2 teaspoons garlic powder
1 teaspoon ground black pepper

Prepare Garlic-Herb Seasoning. Preheat oven to 350F (175C). Cut bread into 16 slices. Arrange in a single layer on a large baking sheet. In a small bowl, blend butter or margarine and 2 teaspoons Garlic-Herb Seasoning. Spread evenly over bread slices. Sprinkle slices with sesame seeds. Bake until hot and crisp, about 15 minutes. Makes 32 appetizer or 8 accompaniment servings.

Garlic-Herb Seasoning:
In a screwtop jar, combine all ingredients. Cover tightly. Shake well. Store in a cool dry place. Also use to flavor cauliflower, broccoli, cabbage or turnips. Makes about 3/4 cup.

Garden Salmon Salad

This hearty salad owes its distinctive flavor to pickled nasturtium seeds.

1 medium cucumber, peeled
1 (15-1/2-oz.) can salmon,
  drained, boned
3 green onions with tops, thinly sliced
2 tablespoons well-drained
  Pickled Nasturtium Seeds, page 35

2 tablespoons lemon juice
Small, young nasturtium leaves,
  washed, patted dry
Mayonnaise
8 cherry tomatoes, halved

Cut cucumber in half lengthwise, then in half crosswise. With the tip of a teaspoon, remove seeds. Cut cucumber halves in paper-thin crosswise slices. In a medium bowl, combine sliced cucumber, salmon, green onions, nasturtium seeds and lemon juice. Toss lightly to blend. Cover and refrigerate until ready to serve. Line a shallow serving bowl with nasturtium leaves. To salmon mixture, add just enough mayonnaise to bind. Spoon over nasturtium leaves. Garnish with tomato halves. Makes 4 servings.

Variation
Substitute 2 tablespoons well-drained capers for Pickled Nasturtium Seeds, and Boston or butter-lettuce leaves for nasturtium leaves.

Honey-Nectarine Brandy

Prepare when the fruit is in season and store away to give as gifts at the holidays.

10 lbs. nectarines, peeled, pitted, diced
6 cups water
5 cups honey
2 (3-inch) cinnamon sticks
1 whole nutmeg

2 tablespoons juniper berries
2 teaspoons whole cloves
2 teaspoons whole allspice
2 qts. brandy

Place nectarines and water in a large saucepan. Bring to a boil. Reduce heat. Simmer, covered, 1 hour. Strain through a fine sieve, pressing with back of a spoon to extract as much fruit pulp as possible. Return liquid to saucepan. Stir in honey, cinnamon, nutmeg, juniper berries, cloves and allspice. Bring to a boil. Reduce heat. Simmer, covered, 30 minutes. Strain; discard spices. Stir in brandy. Pour into sterilized glass bottles; cover tightly. Let stand in a cool, dark, dry place 2 weeks, at which point there will be sediment in the bottoms of the bottles. Pour out clear liquid and reserve. Discard sediment. Wash and sterilize bottles. Refill with brandy liquid; cover tightly. Can be used at any time, but is at its best if let stand at least 2 months. Makes about 3 quarts.

Crisp Benne Thins

Little cookies made with benne seeds, as sesame seeds are often called in the South.

2/3 cup sesame seeds
1/2 cup butter or margarine,
  room temperature
1/2 cup granulated sugar
1/2 cup packed dark-brown sugar

1 egg
1 cup all-purpose flour
1 teaspoon vanilla extract
1/8 teaspoon salt

Preheat oven to 275F (135C). Place sesame seeds in a pie plate. Bake until lightly toasted, stirring occasionally, about 10 minutes. Set aside to cool. Increase oven temperature to 350F (175C). Lightly grease a large baking sheet; set aside. In large bowl of electric mixer, cream butter or margarine, granulated sugar and brown sugar until light and fluffy. Beat in egg. Stir in flour, vanilla, salt and toasted sesame seeds. Drop by rounded 1/2 teaspoons onto prepared baking sheet, about 3 inches apart. Bake in preheated oven until golden brown, 10 to 12 minutes. Let stand 1 minute on baking sheet. Use a metal spatula to place baked cookies on a rack to cool. Cookies can be stored, loosely covered, at room temperature up to 1 week or wrapped airtight and frozen. Makes about 72 cookies.

Buy only enough spices or dried herbs to last for about 3 months. They begin to lose fragrance and pungency, and sometimes color, after that time.

California Poppy-Seed Cake

An airy chiffon cake with the crunch of poppy seeds and the tang of lemon glaze.

1/2 cup poppy seeds
3/4 cup boiling water
7 egg yolks
7 to 8 egg whites
2 cups all-purpose flour
1-1/2 cups sugar

1 tablespoon baking powder
1 teaspoon salt
1/2 cup vegetable oil
2 teaspoons vanilla extract
1/2 teaspoon cream of tartar
Lemon Glaze, see below

Lemon Glaze:
2 tablespoons lemon juice
1 teaspoon grated lemon peel

1 (1-lb.) pkg. powdered sugar, sifted
Cool water as needed

Place poppy seeds in a medium, heatproof bowl. Pour boiling water over seeds. Let stand 2 hours. Separate 7 eggs, placing egg yolks in a small bowl and egg whites in a measuring cup. If 7 egg whites do not measure 1 cup, add enough egg white from remaining egg to make 1 cup. Let stand at room temperature 1 hour. Preheat oven to 325F (165C). In a large bowl, combine flour, sugar, baking powder and salt. Stir with fork or slotted spoon to blend. Use a spoon to make a well in the center of flour mixture. Add in order, oil, egg yolks, poppy seeds with soaking water and vanilla. Using a slotted spoon, beat until blended. Pour egg whites into large bowl of electric mixer. Add cream of tartar. Beat with mixer until soft peaks form. Gradually fold in flour mixture, until no white streaks remain. Pour into an ungreased 10-inch tube pan. Bake in preheated oven until top of cake springs back when gently touched with your fingertips, about 70 minutes. Invert pan, placing neck of a funnel or a large bottle in tube. Let cake hang until completely cooled. Gently slide the blade of a thin knife around outer edge and tube edge to loosen cake from pan. Place a large plate over top of pan. Invert and shake cake to turn it out onto plate. Prepare Lemon Glaze. Slowly pour glaze over cake, letting glaze run down side and into center hole. Makes 14 to 16 servings.

Lemon Glaze:
In a medium bowl, combine lemon juice, lemon peel and powdered sugar. If necessary, add cool water, 1/2 teaspoon at a time, until glaze reaches thick pouring consistency.

Drying Citrus Fruit Peel

Citrus fruit peels—orange, lemon, lime, tangerine, or grapefruit—can be dried at home. If you have a food dehydrator, use it as the manufacturer directs. *To dry peel in the oven:* Preheat oven to 160F (70C). Place a metal rack on a baking sheet. Cover rack with a single layer of cheesecloth; set aside. With your fingers, pull out and discard white membrane from inside of peel. Arrange pieces of peel on prepared rack in a single layer, not touching. Place in oven; prop oven door open about 4 inches. Reduce oven temperature to 140F (60C). Position an electric fan so air flows through open door and over fruit. Change position of fan during drying so peels dry evenly. Turn tray 1/4 turn every 20 minutes. Drying time varies with thickness of peel, size of pieces and moisture content, but should be complete in 3 to 6 hours. Let dried peel cool. Grate peel in a blender or food processor. *To dry grated peel in the sun:* Arrange 2 thicknesses of paper towels on a large baking sheet. Spread grated peel on paper towels. Place in direct sun. Drying takes 1 to 2 days in a steady, hot sun. Store dried peel in small, airtight containers in a cool, dry place.

Three-Cornered Hats

These are the delightful hamantaschen baked for the happy Jewish festival of Purim.

Poppy-Seed Filling, see below
1 (1/4-oz.) pkg. active dry yeast
   (1 tablespoon)
1/2 cup sugar
1/4 cup warm water (110F, 45C)
1/4 cup butter or margarine,
   room temperature

1 teaspoon salt
1 cup milk, scalded
2 eggs, slightly beaten
5 cups all-purpose flour
Cold water
1 egg yolk
1 tablespoon water

Poppy-Seed Filling:
1 cup poppy seeds
1/2 cup milk
1/4 cup honey
2 tablespoons sugar

1/8 teaspoon salt
1 teaspoon lemon juice
1 egg, slightly beaten

Prepare Poppy-Seed Filling; set aside to cool. In a small bowl, stir yeast and 1 tablespoon sugar into warm water. Let stand until bubbly, about 10 minutes. In a large bowl, combine remaining sugar, butter or margarine and salt. Stir in hot milk until butter or margarine melts and sugar dissolves. Stir in yeast mixture, eggs and 2 cups flour. Beat until dough is smooth and falls in sheets when spoon is lifted from bowl. Spoon 2 tablespoons of remaining flour onto a flat surface for kneading. Stir remaining flour into dough. Turn dough out onto floured surface. Clean and grease bowl; set aside. Knead dough to incorporate flour, about 6 minutes. Place dough in bowl, turning to grease all sides. Cover with a dry cloth. Let rise in a warm place, free from drafts, until doubled in bulk, about 2 hours. Punch down dough. Cover and let rest 10 minutes. Preheat oven to 350F (175C). On a lightly floured board, roll dough 1/16 inch thick. Cut into 3-inch circles. Moisten edges with a little water. Place a scant tablespoon of cool Poppy-Seed Filling in center of each circle. Use blunt side of a knife blade to mark edge of dough circles at 3 equidistant points. Bring 2 marked points of circle together over filling, pinching touching edges firmly. Bring up remaining marked point and pinch edges firmly together, forming a triangular pastry. In a small bowl, beat egg yolk and 1 tablespoon water. Brush over tops of pastries. Place on ungreased baking sheets. Bake in preheated oven until browned, 20 to 25 minutes. Place on a rack to cool. Pastries can be stored in containers with tight-fitting lids at room temperature up to 3 days. Or, they can be wrapped airtight and frozen. Makes about 40 filled pastries.

Poppy-Seed Filling:
In a medium saucepan, combine poppy seeds, milk, honey, sugar and salt. Cook over medium heat, stirring constantly, until thickened, about 10 minutes. Stir in lemon juice. Add a little of poppy-seed mixture to egg, stirring vigorously. Stir into remaining poppy-seed mixture. Remove from heat. Cool completely before using. Makes about 2 cups.

Coat fresh cream cheese or mild goats' milk cheese with finely snipped fresh herbs, pressing firmly into cheese on all sides. Enclose snugly in plastic wrap; refrigerate 24 hours. Sage, thyme, basil and fresh coriander (cilantro) are good but you can use any herb you like.

How to Make Three-Cornered Hats

1/Cut dough into 3-inch circles. Mark edge of circles at 3 equidistant points.

2/Bring 2 marked points of circle together over filling, pinching touching edges firmly.

3/Bring up remaining marked point and pinch edges together, making a triangular pastry.

4/Bake on an ungreased sheet until golden brown. Tops will open as pastries cook.

Onion & Pepper Families

Nearly every kitchen has some form of the onion. This close kin of lovely, fragrant lilies and hyacinths is the most common vegetable used for seasonings.

In produce markets, you'll find fresh chives, also called *spring onions;* scallions—more commonly called *green onions;* leeks that look like giant scallions; tiny white pearl onions for pickling; slightly larger ones for boiling; and all-purpose, medium-size white or yellow onions. Yellow onions are actually tan in color and have a stronger flavor than the white ones. Mild, sweet, brown or yellow Spanish onions, white or brown Bermudas and red Italians are all large and slightly flattened.

Shallots are small, lavender-brown-skinned onions that combine the flavor of green onions with just a hint of garlic. When a recipe calls for shallots, you may substitute an equal amount of green onions with a drop or two of garlic juice.

Garlic heads are made up of small bulbs, called *cloves,* that are neatly arranged in a chrysanthemum-like cluster. Garlic's strong flavor is diminished by cooking.

Plump, sweet red or green bell peppers are the most popular peppers for seasoning. However, with the interest in Mexican cookery, various peppers, called *chilies,* have become popular. Chilies range in flavor from mildly spicy to *extremely* hot. They are available fresh, dried or canned in water or vinegar. Pickled chilies are labeled *en escabeche.*

There are two things to keep in mind when using fresh chilies: If the flesh of the pepper is hot, the seeds will be hotter. Wear rubber gloves when working with them in quantity—they can give you as nasty a burn as scalding water.

Bright green *Anaheim* chilies are the mildest. Most canned whole or chopped chilies are Anaheims. *Poblanos* are relatively mild, with shiny green-black skins. *Jalapeños* are hot, with smooth, dark-green skins. *Serranos* are the hottest of the fresh chilies widely available. They have dark-green skins. Jalapeños and serranos are available fresh or pickled.

Pulverized dried peppers combined with cumin, oregano and seasonings make up *chili powder.* It can vary in strength from mild to hot. *Red pepper,* formerly labeled *cayenne,* is made from pulverized hot-pepper flesh and seeds. No salt or sugar is added. It's good in egg dishes. *Paprika* is also made from pulverized peppers.

Menu

Company-Coming Dinner: Summer

Summertime Salad, page 54
Chicken Breasts Hungarian-Style, page 57
Celery & Parsley Noodles
Elegant Eggplant, page 115
Braised Endive
Fresh Lemon Ice Cream
Chilled Rosé Wine
After-Dinner Espresso

Lumpensuppe

Known in Germany as hangover soup, it's delicious for sober citizens as well.

3 tablespoons butter or margarine
1-1/2 cups thinly sliced onions
6 cups Beef Stock, page 98,
  or canned beef broth
1/4 teaspoon ground black pepper

1 cup dry red wine
6 slices toasted French bread
1/2 cup grated Parmesan cheese (1-1/2 oz.)
1/2 cup shredded Gruyère cheese (2 oz.)

In a 2-quart saucepan, melt butter or margarine over medium heat. Add onions. Stirring frequently, sauté until onions are a rich golden brown. Add stock or broth. Bring to a boil. Reduce heat to low. Cover and simmer 25 minutes. Preheat oven to 275F (135C). Add pepper and wine to onion mixture. Simmer 10 minutes. Divide soup among 6 ovenproof serving dishes. Float a slice of toast on each. Combine cheeses and sprinkle evenly over toast. Bake in preheated oven until cheese is softened, 5 to 7 minutes. Serve immediately. Makes 6 servings.

Tuna Loaf with Chervil Butter

The butter mixture adds moisture and flavor to this family-style dish.

Chervil Butter, page 111
2 (12-oz.) cans chunk-style tuna
3 cups fresh white breadcrumbs
1-1/2 cups milk
2 eggs, slightly beaten
1 medium onion, grated

2 celery stalks, minced
1/2 teaspoon salt
1/4 teaspoon ground white pepper
2 tablespoons lemon juice
2 tablespoons minced fresh parsley
Parsley sprigs, if desired

Prepare Chervil Butter; refrigerate. Preheat oven to 350F (175C). Grease a 9" x 5" loaf pan; set aside. In a large bowl, combine tuna and breadcrumbs. Combine milk and eggs. Add to tuna mixture. Add onion, celery, salt, pepper, lemon juice and minced parsley. Mix gently. Spoon into prepared pan. Bake in preheated oven until just firm, 45 to 55 minutes. Cool in pan 5 minutes, then invert onto a hot platter. Garnish with parsley sprigs, if desired. To serve, cut into slices. Top each slice with a dollop of Chervil Butter. Makes 8 servings.

Roasted Garlic

An absolutely delicious and surprisingly mild-flavored appetizer or snack.

1 cup olive oil
8 whole garlic heads
1 teaspoon salt

1/4 teaspoon ground black pepper
1 (1-lb.) round loaf dark pumpernickel bread,
torn into 8 pieces

Preheat oven to 200F (95C). Use 1 tablespoon olive oil to grease bottom of an 8-inch square baking pan; set aside. Make a shallow incision all around each garlic head, halfway between top and bottom, cutting through the skin but not into meat of garlic. Lift off pointed top of each head. Arrange garlic in prepared pan. Pour remaining olive oil over garlic heads. Sprinkle with salt and pepper. Bake, uncovered, in preheated oven 15 minutes. Cover pan with foil and continue baking 1 hour or until garlic is tender. Serve warm, letting each person spread some of soft garlic on a piece of bread. Makes 8 servings.

Cock-a-Leekie

Easy-do version of a hearty, old-country soup to serve hot or chilled.

6 large leeks
3 cups water
1-1/2 teaspoons salt
1-1/2 cups Chicken Stock, page 98,
**   or canned chicken broth**

1/8 teaspoon ground nutmeg
2 tablespoons chicken fat,
**   butter or margarine**
1/2 cup whipping cream
Salt and ground white pepper to taste

Remove roots and all dark-green portions from tops of leeks. Wash under running water to remove any sand or dirt. Cut each leek in half lengthwise, then crosswise into 1/8-inch slices. In a large saucepan, bring water to a boil over medium-high heat. Add 1-1/2 teaspoons salt and sliced leeks. Bring back to a boil. Reduce heat to low. Cover and simmer until leeks are tender, 5 to 7 minutes. Add stock or broth, nutmeg and chicken fat, butter or margarine. Bring to a boil over medium-high heat. Reduce heat to low. Gradually stir in cream. Cook only until heated through. Season to taste with salt and white pepper. Serve hot or cold. Makes 5 to 6 servings.

Variations

Add 1 to 1-1/2 cups diced cooked chicken after adding cream.

To follow original recipe, add 3/4 cup diced, pitted prunes after adding cream.

How to Make Roasted Garlic

1/Around center of each head of garlic, make a shallow incision, cutting through skin only.

2/Lift off top of each head, leaving clusters of cloves intact. Arrange in prepared pan.

Fresh Chili Sauce

This is the Salsa Fresca that no Mexican table would be without. It's best on meat or cheese dishes.

1 cup finely chopped ripe tomato
1/2 cup chopped onion
1/4 cup snipped fresh coriander (cilantro)
1 teaspoon salt

1 teaspoon vinegar
1 small yellow wax chili or
** 1 small jalapeño pepper**

In a small bowl, combine tomato, onion, coriander, salt and vinegar; set aside. Remove seeds and membrane from pepper. Chop finely and stir into tomato mixture. Let stand at room temperature 5 hours or more before serving to give flavors time to blend. Makes about 1-3/4 cups.

Variation
If you cannot find fresh yellow wax or jalapeño peppers, substitute 1 small canned jalapeño pepper, labeled *hot peppers* or *jalapeños en escabeche*. These are not the same product, but either will give you the desirable hot-pepper flavor. Regulate the hotness of your salsa by the amount of pepper you use.

Garlic Soup

Sopa de Ajo, a suppertime standby in many Spanish-speaking countries.

1-1/2 qts. Veal Stock or Chicken Stock,
   page 98, or canned chicken broth
2 tablespoons olive oil
12 garlic cloves, peeled
6 thin slices firm bread,
   cut in small cubes

1/2 teaspoon red (cayenne) pepper
Salt to taste
6 eggs
6 small sprigs fresh coriander
   (cilantro)

In a 4-quart saucepan, heat stock or broth over low heat. In a medium skillet, heat oil over medium-low heat. Add garlic to oil. Sauté until golden brown. Watch carefully so garlic does not burn. Use a slotted spoon to place browned garlic in hot stock or broth. Add bread cubes to skillet. Sauté until golden brown. With slotted spoon, place in hot stock or broth. Stir in red pepper. Season with salt to taste. Bring to a boil over medium-high heat. Reduce heat to low; simmer 6 minutes. Break 1 egg into each of 6 soup bowls. Lightly beat each egg. Pour hot soup over egg, stirring gently with a fork. Garnish with coriander sprig. Serve immediately. Makes 6 servings.

Italian Sausage & Pepper

Coupled with the cheese-rich potato puff, this makes a hearty cold-weather dinner.

Parmesan-Potato Puff, see below
8 large Italian sausages, sweet or hot
1 large onion, sliced

3 green bell peppers, cut in strips
Salt and ground black pepper to taste
2 tablespoons snipped fresh parsley

Parmesan-Potato Puff:
3 large russet potatoes, peeled, diced
1/4 cup butter or margarine
3 tablespoons half and half

Salt and ground white pepper
4 eggs, separated
2/3 cup grated Parmesan cheese (2 oz.)

Prepare Parmesan-Potato Puff. While Puff bakes, prick each sausage in 3 places with a sharp fork. Place in a cold large skillet. Over medium-low heat, cook sausages slowly, turning frequently, until cooked through and browned. Remove from skillet and keep warm. Discard all but 3 tablespoons fat from skillet. Add onion and green pepper. Cook and stir over medium heat until crisp-tender and lightly browned. Season to taste with salt and pepper. Add cooked sausages. Cook 5 minutes longer. To serve, sprinkle with parsley. Serve with hot Parmesan-Potato Puff. Makes 4 to 6 servings.

Parmesan-Potato Puff:
Cook potatoes in boiling salted water until tender; drain well. Preheat oven to 350F (175C). Lightly grease a shallow 1-1/2-quart baking dish; set aside. In a small saucepan, heat butter or margarine with half and half until melted. Mash potatoes. Beat in half and half mixture. Season to taste with salt and white pepper. In a small bowl, beat egg yolks slightly. Stir into potato mixture. Stir in cheese. In a medium bowl, beat egg whites until stiff but not dry. Gently fold into potato mixture. Spread evenly in prepared pan. Bake in preheated oven until puffy and golden brown, about 45 minutes. Serve immediately.

Lancaster Green Salad

Lettuce and spinach the down-home way with hot dressing and bacon.

Lancaster County Dressing, see below
1/2 lb. thick-sliced bacon
1 large head iceberg lettuce

1/4 lb. fresh spinach, washed, drained
Milk

Prepare Lancaster County Dressing. In a large skillet, cook bacon until crisp. Drain on paper towels. Tear lettuce into bite-size pieces. Remove heavy stems from spinach. Tear leaves into bite-size pieces. Combine lettuce and spinach. Arrange on a large platter. Pour off all but about 1/4 cup bacon fat from skillet. Add 1-1/2 cups Lancaster County Dressing. Stir constantly over very low heat until fat is incorporated into dressing. If needed, thin dressing with a little milk to the consistency of lightly whipped cream. Continue to cook until dressing is heated through. Spoon over greens on platter. Break bacon into 1-inch pieces. Sprinkle over platter. Serve immediately. Makes 6 servings.

Lancaster County Dressing

Use this old-fashioned dressing for both side-dish and main-dish salads.

2 eggs
3/4 cup sugar
5 tablespoons granular instant flour
1/2 teaspoon garlic juice
1 tablespoon onion juice

1 teaspoon dry mustard
3/4 teaspoon ground turmeric
1 cup cider vinegar
2 cups milk

Break eggs into a heavy saucepan. Beat with a whisk until whites and yolks are combined. Add sugar, flour, garlic and onion juices, mustard and turmeric. Whisk until blended. Gradually add vinegar, whisking constantly. Whisk in milk. Cook over very low heat, stirring frequently, until mixture bubbles and thickens, about 15 minutes. Cool. Cover tightly and store in refrigerator up to 3 weeks. Makes about 3 cups.

Variations
Reduce amount of sugar in this dressing, depending on the use you wish to make of it. For example, use only 3 tablespoons sugar in dressing for potato salad or egg salad. Dressing may be used hot or cold; in either case, thin to desired consistency with milk.

When working with hot peppers, wear rubber gloves. Cut the peppers under cold running water to protect hands and eyes from juices and fumes.

Party Peppers

A platter of these savory stuffed peppers makes a delicious addition to a buffet.

6 red bell peppers
6 green bell peppers
Savory Stuffing, see below

3 tablespoons olive oil
24 rolled anchovy fillets with capers
Fresh parsley sprigs

Savory Stuffing:
2 tablespoons olive oil
4 green onions, minced
3/4 teaspoon garlic juice
3 slices prosciutto ham, minced
7 anchovy fillets, minced
1/3 cup finely chopped shelled
   pistachio nuts
1-1/2 cups fresh breadcrumbs
1/3 cup whipping cream

1 egg, slightly beaten
2 tablespoons grated Romano cheese
1/4 teaspoon dried leaf oregano,
   crumbled
1/4 teaspoon dried leaf marjoram,
   crumbled
1 tablespoon snipped fresh parsley
1/2 teaspoon salt
1/4 teaspoon ground black pepper

Preheat broiler, if required. Broil peppers, turning 2 or 3 times, until just charred on each side. Use kitchen tongs to place in a plastic bag. Close bag tightly. Let stand 5 minutes. Use a knife to pull peel from peppers. Cut each pepper in half lengthwise. Discard stems and seeds. Rinse in cold water. Pat dry with paper towels; set aside. Prepare Savory Stuffing. Brush a large shallow baking dish with 1 tablespoon oil. Divide stuffing among pepper halves. Bring long sides of peppers to center, over stuffing. Place seam-side down in prepared pan. Brush peppers with remaining 2 tablespoons oil. Cover and let stand at room temperature 4 hours, or refrigerate overnight. Preheat oven to 375F (190C). If peppers have been refrigerated, let come to room temperature. Bake until heated through, about 30 minutes. Carefully transfer to a platter. Top each pepper half with an anchovy fillet. Garnish with parsley sprigs. Serve hot or at room temperature. Makes 12 servings.

Savory Stuffing
In a large saucepan, heat oil over medium heat. Add green onions. Cook 2 minutes. Add garlic juice, prosciutto, anchovy fillets and nuts. Cook and stir 2 minutes. Increase heat slightly. Add breadcrumbs. Cook, stirring constantly, until lightly browned, 3 to 4 minutes. Add cream, 1 tablespoon at a time, stirring until absorbed. Turn mixture into a medium bowl. Cool 15 minutes. Stir in remaining ingredients.

Summertime Salad

The paprika vinaigrette serves as both dressing and marinade.

1/3 cup white-wine vinegar
1 tablespoon grated onion
2 teaspoons sweet paprika
1/4 teaspoon salt
2/3 cup olive oil or vegetable oil

3 ripe tomatoes, sliced
1 large cucumber, thinly sliced
2 green bell peppers, cut in thin strips
1/2 lb. mushrooms, thinly sliced
Watercress sprigs

In a screwtop jar, combine vinegar, onion, paprika and salt. Cover tightly. Shake well. Add oil, cover and shake again; set aside. On a shallow platter with a rim, arrange tomatoes, cucumber, peppers and mushrooms. Shake dressing again. Slowly pour over vegetables. Refrigerate until 30 minutes before serving. Garnish with watercress sprigs. Makes 6 servings.

How to Make Party Peppers

1/Broil peppers, just until charred on each side. Use tongs to place in a plastic bag. After 5 minutes, peel peppers.

2/Spoon stuffing into peeled pepper halves. Fold long sides of peppers over stuffing. Place seam-side down in pan.

British Boiled Beef

Hearty, richly flavorful change-of-pace dish for family or guests.

3 tablespoons bacon fat or vegetable oil	1 Bouquet Garni, page 133
1 cup chopped onion	1 teaspoon salt
1 (3-lb.) beef brisket	2 cups boiling water
	Horseradish Cream, page 105

In a Dutch oven or heavy pot, heat fat or oil over medium heat. Add onion. Stirring occasionally, cook until lightly browned. Add beef, Bouquet Garni and salt. Pour in water. Bring just to boiling point. Reduce heat to low. Simmer, covered, until tender, about 2-1/2 hours. Place cooked beef on a hot platter; cooking liquid can be used as beef stock. Let beef stand 10 minutes. Prepare Horseradish Cream. Cut beef across grain into thin slices. Serve immediately. Pass Horseradish Cream separately. Makes 6 servings.

Seafood Salad Rémoulade

A classic salad of crab and shrimp, crowned with a classic dressing.

1/2 cucumber, peeled
3 celery stalks,
    cut in thin diagonal slices
1/2 teaspoon salt
1 lb. lump crabmeat
1/2 lb. deveined cooked tiny bay shrimp

2 tablespoons grated onion
Salt and ground white pepper
Rémoulade Sauce, page 102
3 hard-cooked eggs, shelled
3 small tomatoes
1 bunch watercress

Cut cucumber in half lengthwise. Use the tip of a teaspoon to remove seeds. Cut halves into 1/8-inch slices. In a medium saucepan, combine cucumber slices, celery and 1/2 teaspoon salt. Add cold water to cover. Bring to a boil over medium-high heat. Immediately drain. Refrigerate vegetables. Pick over crabmeat, removing tendons and pieces of shell. In a medium bowl, combine crabmeat, shrimp, cooled vegetables and grated onion. Sprinkle lightly with salt and white pepper. Gently toss with 2 forks. Prepare Rémoulade Sauce. Serve salad immediately, or refrigerate. To serve, cut eggs and tomatoes into quarters. Line a platter with watercress. Spoon crabmeat mixture in center. Surround with eggs and tomatoes. Spoon sauce over top. Serve immediately. Makes 6 servings.

Sutter's Mill Chicken

Serve with fresh, hot corn bread for a country-style meal.

1 (2-1/2-lb.) broiler-fryer chicken,
    cut in serving pieces
1 teaspoon salt
3 tablespoons butter or margarine
1 large onion, halved, thinly sliced

2 teaspoons chili powder
1/2 cup golden raisins
1 cup whipping cream
2 (10-oz.) pkgs. frozen spinach,
    cooked, drained

Sprinkle chicken with salt. In a large, heavy skillet with ovenproof handle, heat butter or margarine over medium heat until bubbly. Add dark-meat chicken pieces. Sauté 5 minutes. Add white-meat pieces. Continue to sauté until all chicken is golden brown. Drain chicken on paper towels. Preheat oven to 300F (150C). Discard all but 2 tablespoons fat from skillet. Add onion to skillet. Cook until tender but not browned. Stir in chili powder and raisins. Return browned chicken to skillet. Spoon onion mixture over chicken, then pour cream evenly over chicken. Do not cover skillet. Bake in preheated oven until tender, about 1 hour. Turn chicken once during baking. Spread hot spinach around edge of a platter. Arrange chicken in center. Pour sauce evenly over chicken. Makes 4 servings.

Chicken Breasts Hungarian-Style

Lecsó, a piquant Hungarian pepper sauce, adds zest to this or any other bland meat dish.

2 to 2-1/2 cups Lecsó, see below
6 large chicken-breast halves,
    boned, skinned
Salt and ground white pepper
6 small zucchini, cut in half lengthwise

6 small yellow crookneck squash,
    cut in half lengthwise
1-1/2 cups coarsely shredded Muenster
    cheese (6 oz.)

Lecsó:
1/2 cup vegetable oil
6 cups coarsely chopped onions
    (8 medium)
1/2 lb. lean bacon, cut in large dice
4 cups peeled, seeded,
    coarsely chopped tomatoes (6 large)
9 large green bell peppers,
    coarsely chopped

1 red bell pepper, coarsely chopped
1 large garlic clove, minced
1 tablespoon sweet paprika
1 teaspoon salt
1/2 teaspoon sugar
1/4 teaspoon ground caraway seeds
1/8 teaspoon red (cayenne) pepper

Prepare Lecsó. Preheat oven to 325F (165C). Lightly grease a large, shallow baking dish. Place chicken breasts in baking dish. Sprinkle lightly with salt and pepper. Arrange zucchini and crookneck squash around and between chicken pieces. Cover pan tightly with foil. Bake in preheated oven until chicken is opaque and tender when pierced with a fork, and vegetables are crisp-tender, about 30 minutes. Remove foil. Spoon Lecsó over chicken and vegetables. Bake, uncovered, 10 minutes longer. Sprinkle with cheese. Bake until cheese softens, 3 to 5 minutes. Serve immediately. Makes 6 servings.

Lecsó:
In a Dutch oven, heat oil over medium heat. Add onions and bacon. Cook, stirring frequently, until lightly browned. Stir in remaining ingredients. Reduce heat to low. Stirring frequently, simmer, uncovered, until vegetables are tender and sauce is thickened, 30 to 40 minutes. Lecsó may be covered and stored in the refrigerator up to 7 days. Makes about 6 cups.

Amounts of Herbs To Use

Frozen herbs require about twice the amount you would use of the fresh herb. Those stored **in vinegar or oil** can be used in the same amounts as the fresh herb. When you substitute **fresh herbs** in a recipe that calls for the **dried** variety, use 1 tablespoon of the fresh herb for each 1/2 to 1 teaspoon of the dried. In using any herbs, add some, taste, and add more if you wish.

To peel onions, particularly small ones in some quantity, place in a saucepan, cover with cold water and bring to a boil. Boil 1 minute. Cool and peel—the skins will slip off easily.

Foot-of-the-Mountain Snack Cheese

The Piedmontese swear this snack will fend off the Angel of Death.

1 cup ricotta cheese (8 oz.)	**3/4 teaspoon salt**
1/2 cup crumbled Gorgonzola cheese (2 oz.)	**2 fresh geranium leaves**
1 large garlic head, separated in cloves, unpeeled	**1/3 cup finely chopped walnuts or pecans**
1 cup whipping cream	**Assorted crackers**
	Celery sticks, turnip wedges, cucumber slices, zucchini slices

About 30 minutes before preparing snack, remove both cheeses from refrigerator and bring to room temperature. Line a 4-cup strainer with cheesecloth; set aside. Place garlic cloves in a small saucepan. Add water to cover. Bring to a boil over high heat. Reduce heat to medium. Cook until garlic can be easily pierced with tip of a sharp knife, 15 to 20 minutes. Drain well. Press garlic through a small strainer or garlic press to puree. Reserve 2 tablespoons; set aside. Use remaining garlic puree for another cooked dish requiring garlic. In a medium bowl, beat ricotta cheese until softened. Add Gorgonzola and beat until smooth. Gradually beat in cream. Stir in salt and 2 tablespoons reserved garlic puree. Cut an 18" x 12" piece of cheesecloth. Dampen, then wring out as dry as possible. In center of dampened cheesecloth, place geranium leaves, top-side down. Spoon cheese mixture over leaves. Shape into a ball. Bring sides of cheesecloth together around cheese. Tie cheesecloth edges together with string close to cheese ball. Place in prepared strainer. Place strainer over a medium bowl. Refrigerate at least 24 hours or as long as 4 days. Gently peel away cheesecloth and leaves. Place cheese ball on a serving dish. Firmly press nuts into surface of cheese. Let stand at room temperature 1 hour before serving with assorted crackers and vegetables. Makes about 2 cups.

Variation
If fresh geranium leaves are not available, substitute 2 small sage or nasturtium leaves.

Fresh Coriander Dip

Pretty, delicious, easy appetizer—what more could you ask?

1 cup firmly packed fresh coriander (cilantro)	**1/4 teaspoon ground cumin**
3 canned jalapeño peppers en escabeche, seeded	**1/8 teaspoon sugar**
	3 cups small corn chips
2 large garlic cloves, chopped	**1/2 large jícama, peeled, cut in small finger shapes**
2 tablespoons plain yogurt	
1 tablespoon lemon juice	**1/2 fresh pineapple, peeled, cored, cut in small finger shapes**

In blender, combine coriander, peppers, garlic and yogurt. Process at medium speed until pureed, about 1 minute. Add lemon juice, cumin and sugar; process 30 seconds. Spoon into a serving dish. Let stand at room temperature 30 minutes to blend flavors. When ready to serve, place dish of dip on a platter. Arrange chips, jícama and pineapple around dip. Makes 3/4 cup dip, or about 14 appetizer servings.

Foot-of-the-Mountain Snack Cheese garnished with Geranium leaves.

59

Feast for a Dozen Garlic-Lovers

Aioli is a superb garlicky sauce from the south of France.

Aioli, page 106
2 qts. water
2 medium onions, sliced
12 black peppercorns
4 whole allspice
1/3 cup lemon juice
3 bay leaves
2 teaspoons salt
1 cup white-wine vinegar
6 lbs. ling-cod or rockfish fillets
3 tablespoons vegetable oil
8 green onions, sliced
Salt and pepper to taste

Shrimp in Wine Sauce, see below
12 small whole unpeeled potatoes,
  cooked, drained
12 large whole carrots, cooked, drained
2 lbs. whole green beans, cooked, drained
2 medium heads cauliflower,
  broken into flowerets, cooked, drained
3 (10-oz.) pkgs. frozen artichoke hearts,
  cooked, drained
1 loaf crusty whole-wheat French or
  Italian bread
Green or ripe olives
Oil-processed ripe olives

Shrimp in Wine Sauce:
2 tablespoons olive oil
1 small onion, chopped
2 garlic cloves, minced
1 bay leaf
1/2 teaspoon dried leaf thyme

2 lbs. deveined shelled raw shrimp,
  fresh or frozen
1 tablespoon tomato paste
1/2 cup dry white wine
Salt and pepper to taste

Prepare Aioli. In a large saucepan, combine water, sliced onions, peppercorns, allspice, lemon juice, bay leaves, 2 teaspoons salt and vinegar. Bring to a boil over high heat. Reduce heat to low. Cover and simmer 30 minutes. Preheat oven to 425F (220C). Grease a very large or 2 smaller baking pans. Arrange fish fillets in a single layer in pan or pans. Strain liquid over fish. Add hot water as needed to cover fish. Cover tightly. Bake until fish is opaque throughout, 12 to 20 minutes. Place on a large platter with a raised rim; keep warm. Reserve cooking liquid. Pour vegetable oil into a large skillet. Add green onions. Cook over medium heat, stirring, until tender but not browned. Add 1/2 cup reserved cooking liquid. Refrigerate remaining cooking liquid; use for other fish sauces. Bring onion mixture to a boil. Add salt and pepper to taste. Pour over fish. Prepare Shrimp in Wine Sauce; keep warm. If vegetables were cooked ahead and refrigerated, reheat them by plunging each briefly into boiling salted water. If they were just cooked, serve them warm or at room temperature. To serve, place vegetables in individual dishes. Cut through bread at 1-inch intervals, not cutting through bottom crust. Set out olives and Aioli in serving dishes. Let each diner help himself, dipping any or all food in the Aioli. Makes 12 servings.

Shrimp in Wine Sauce:
In a large skillet, combine olive oil, chopped onion and garlic. Cook over low heat until soft, but not browned. Add bay leaf, thyme and shrimp. Cook and stir until shrimp just turns pink. With a slotted spoon, place shrimp in a serving dish. Add tomato paste and wine to skillet. Stir over high heat until slightly thickened, about 3 minutes. Discard bay leaf. Season to taste with salt and pepper. Pour over shrimp; toss to coat.

Pork Paprikash

Serve with hot noodles tossed with butter and caraway seeds.

1-1/2 lbs. boneless pork shoulder	3/4 teaspoon salt
1 large white onion, sliced	2 tablespoons sweet paprika
2 tablespoons vegetable oil	1 cup dairy sour cream
1 tablespoon butter or margarine	2 tablespoons all-purpose flour
1/2 lb. mushrooms, sliced	1 tablespoon snipped fresh parsley
1 cup hot water	

Cut away and discard all visible fat from pork. Cut pork into 1-inch cubes. Gently separate onion slices into rings. In a 6-quart Dutch oven, heat oil and butter or margarine. Add pork and onion rings. Stirring frequently, cook over medium-low heat until lightly browned. Add mushrooms; cook 5 minutes longer. Stir in water and salt. Reduce heat to low; simmer 30 minutes. Stir in 1 tablespoon paprika. Continue to simmer until pork is tender when pierced with a fork, about 25 minutes; add a little more water during cooking if necessary. In a small bowl, combine sour cream, remaining 1 tablespoon paprika and flour. Slowly stir into pork mixture. Cook and stir until mixture bubbles and thickens. Serve immediately, or refrigerate overnight for a richer flavor. Reheat in covered pan over low heat, stirring occasionally. Sprinkle with parsley. Makes 6 servings.

Salad Medley with Shallot Dressing

Shallots lend a delicate not-quite-onion, not-quite-garlic flavor.

Shallot Dressing, see below	3/4 cup diced celery
1/2 lb. mushrooms, sliced	2 large boiling potatoes, cooked,
1 (10-oz.) pkg. frozen cut green beans,	peeled, cubed
cooked, drained	Boston lettuce leaves
2 Granny Smith or other tart apples,	Watercress sprigs
peeled, diced	

Shallot Dressing:

1/4 cup white-wine vinegar	1-1/2 teaspoons Dijon-style mustard
3/4 cup vegetable oil	2 shallots, peeled, quartered
1/2 teaspoon salt	

Prepare Shallot Dressing. In a medium bowl, combine mushrooms, green beans, apples, celery and potatoes. Pour Shallot Dressing over mixture. Toss lightly. Cover and refrigerate about 3 hours. To serve, place lettuce leaves on each of 6 salad plates. With a slotted spoon, stir salad mixture gently, then spoon evenly over lettuce. Garnish each salad with a watercress sprig. Makes 6 servings.

Shallot Dressing:
In blender, combine all ingredients. Process until smooth. Dressing recipe can be doubled. Use 1 cup for salad. Place leftover dressing in a screwtop jar and refrigerate. Use on tossed salads. Makes about 1 cup.

Extracts, Fruit Juices & Peels

Barks, nuts, pods, seeds, flowers, vegetables, fruits and berries all contribute their flavors to extracts. These are made by removing the essential oil and dissolving it in alcohol. The resulting concentrated liquids are used in small amounts—generally from 1/2 teaspoon to 1 tablespoon—to flavor foods, particularly desserts. They hold their flavor through the heat of baking and the cold of refrigerating and freezing.

Those most commonly used are almond, banana, cherry, maple, lemon, orange, rum and vanilla, plus others. They can be found on most supermarket shelves.

Why use extracts? *Convenience:* In a household where rum is not used, rum extract takes its place. *Volume:* It takes a good deal of lemon juice, perhaps enough to over-dilute the food, to produce the flavor of 1/2 teaspoon lemon extract. *Color:* Specks of vanilla bean or nutmeg may be unattractive in a pale-colored food. *Diet:* Butter-flavor extract gives a buttery flavor to foods in which low- or no-cholesterol fats are used.

When measuring extracts, tread lightly and follow the recipe. A small amount of banana extract gives excellent banana flavor, but an excess amount can ruin the dish. Too much almond is bitter rather than delicious. However, if you are very fond of vanilla, add half again as much as the recipe calls for to get a richer flavor.

In choosing extracts, pure is generally better than artificial flavoring. Pure vanilla is far superior to vanillin or other vanilla substitutes. Pineapple and black walnut are two exceptions.

Strength and flavor of extracts dissipates with age. Don't buy more than you'll use in two or three months.

Often fresh fruit flavor is preferable to an extract. Juices can be prepared from fresh fruit, frozen juice concentrates and juice drink concentrates. Frozen or bottled lemon or lime juice is used undiluted. Lemons are the most versatile of the fruits whose juices and peels we use in cooking. A squeeze of lemon makes almost any food sing. Glacéed or dried citrus peel preserves flavorful oils. It is an excellent substitute for fresh-grated peel. Commercially dried citron, grapefruit, lemon and orange are available in strips or grated forms. Glacé citrus peel contains a higher concentration of sugar than the natural fruit. It is used primarily in desserts such as fruitcakes. It is also enjoyed as a confection.

Menu

Sunday Brunch for a Crowd

Mimosa Cocktails & Bloody Marys
Fresh Fruit Platter
Farm-Style Sausage Patties, page 37
Baked Eggs
Buckwheat Cakes, page 68
Spicy Tomato Conserve, page 150

Spiced Cream Twists, page 18
Walnut Muffins with Maple Butter, page 118
Melon-Marmalade Medley, page 66
Crisp Benne Thins, page 44
Mocha Mousse In No Time, page 83
Hot Coffee

Stir-Fry Scallops & Mushrooms

Delicate seasonings enhance, but do not mask, the rich flavor of the scallops.

3 tablespoons vegetable oil
1/2 teaspoon butter-flavor extract
1 small onion, thinly sliced
2 celery stalks, cut in thin diagonal slices
1/2 lb. mushrooms, thinly sliced

1 lb. sea scallops, halved vertically
1/2 teaspoon ginger extract
1/2 teaspoon sherry extract
1/4 cup whipping cream
Salt and ground white pepper to taste

In a large heavy skillet, heat oil over medium heat. Stir in butter-flavor extract. Add onion and celery. Cook and stir until crisp-tender. Add mushrooms and scallops. Cook and stir until scallops are white and opaque, 4 to 6 minutes. In a small bowl, combine ginger extract, sherry extract and cream. Stir into scallop mixture. Stir gently until heated through, about 3 minutes. Season to taste with salt and pepper. Makes 4 servings.

Variations
If ginger extract is not available, substitute 1/2 teaspoon ground ginger.
If sherry extract is not available, substitute 1 to 2 tablespoons sherry.

California-Style Pork Loin

Roast pork, moist and tender—plus the tart-sweetness of orange.

1 (2-1/2-lb.) center-cut pork loin roast
3 navel oranges
2 cups orange juice
1 tablespoon cornstarch

1 tablespoon fresh lemon juice
1/2 teaspoon salt
1/8 teaspoon ground black pepper
1/2 cup cold water

Preheat oven to 375F (190C). Place pork on a rack in a shallow roasting pan. Insert meat thermometer into thickest part of meat, but away from bone. Roast in preheated oven until thermometer registers 165F (75C), about 1-1/4 hours. Cut off colored portion (zest) from 2 oranges, being careful not to include any white pith. Cut zest into fine strips. Place in a small saucepan. Add hot water to cover. Bring to a boil over medium heat. Boil gently 10 minutes. Drain well; set aside. Peel all oranges, removing all white pith. Quarter peeled oranges lengthwise; set aside. In a small saucepan, combine orange juice, cornstarch and lemon juice. Stir until blended. Cook over low heat, stirring occasionally, until thickened, about 5 minutes. Remove from heat. Stir in salt, pepper and cooked orange zest. Set aside and keep warm. Place roasted pork on a warm platter. Pour 1/2 cup cold water into roasting pan. Stir over low heat, scraping up brown bits that cling to pan. Skim off fat and spoon it into a medium skillet. Add orange wedges to fat in skillet. Cook over medium heat until heated through, 3 to 5 minutes. Use a slotted spoon to arrange hot orange wedges around pork on platter. Stir remaining liquid in roasting pan into thickened orange-juice mixture. Spoon over pork and orange wedges. Makes 6 servings.

Leeward Islands Game Hens

If the hens are frozen, ask butcher to halve them with his electric saw.

2 to 3 tablespoons vegetable oil
1 large onion, cut in large cubes
3 garlic cloves, minced
2 Cornish game hens, halved lengthwise
1 cup orange juice
1/2 cup grapefruit juice
1-1/2 teaspoons ground ginger
1/4 cup golden raisins

2 tablespoons sliced ripe olives
1/2 teaspoon salt
1 firm ripe papaya, peeled, seeded,
  cut into large cubes
1 tablespoon cornstarch
2 tablespoons water
1 ripe avocado
1/4 cup toasted sliced almonds

In a deep, 12-inch skillet, heat 2 tablespoons oil over low heat. Add onion and garlic. Cook and stir until onion is soft and just begining to turn golden, about 10 minutes. With a slotted spoon, remove onion and garlic. Place in a small bowl. Add more oil to skillet, if needed. Arrange hens in skillet, skin-side down. Turning several times, cook until golden brown, 15 to 20 minutes. Add cooked onion and garlic, orange juice, grapefruit juice, ginger, raisins, olives and salt. Place papaya pieces on top of hens. Cover. Bring to a boil. Reduce heat to low. Simmer until juices of hens between leg and body run clear when hens are pierced with a fork, about 25 minutes. Arrange hens and papaya on a warm platter; keep warm. Skim off and discard fat from juices in skillet. Stir together cornstarch and water until smooth. Stir into simmering juices in skillet. Cook and stir until thickened. Pour juices, with onion, raisins and olives, over hens and papaya. Peel and slice avocado. Arrange slices around hens. Sprinkle almonds over dish. Serve immediately. Makes 4 servings.

Greek-Style Rice

Serve this lemony rice-and-spinach side dish with broiled or roasted chicken.

1/4 lb. fresh spinach
2 tablespoons olive oil or vegetable oil
2 tablespoons finely chopped onion
3 tablespoons lemon juice

1 cup uncooked brown rice
1/4 teaspoon salt
1-3/4 cups hot water

Wash spinach, drain. Snip off and discard any heavy stems. Chop spinach leaves; set aside. In a medium skillet, heat oil over medium-low heat. Add onion. Cook until soft but not browned. Add lemon juice, rice, salt and water. Bring to a boil. Reduce heat to low. Simmer, covered, until rice is tender, about 45 minutes. Stir in spinach. Serve immediately. Makes 4 servings.

Tamiami Beef Medley

Grapefruit juice works double magic, tenderizing and adding great flavor.

1 cup grapefruit juice
1 teaspoon salt
1 garlic clove, minced
1-1/2 lbs. beef round, cut in 1-inch cubes
2 tablespoons vegetable oil
1 large green bell pepper,
   cut in thin strips

1 large onion, sliced
1 cup chopped fresh tomato
2 tablespoons brown sugar
1 tablespoon red-wine vinegar
1 teaspoon dried leaf rosemary, crumbled
1 bay leaf
1/2 cup sliced ripe olives

In a large bowl, combine grapefruit juice, salt and garlic. Add beef cubes. Cover and refrigerate overnight. In a large heavy skillet, heat oil over medium heat. Drain beef cubes, reserving marinade. Pat beef dry with paper towels. Brown beef in hot oil, turning to brown all sides. Add green pepper and onion. Cook 3 minutes. Stir in tomato. To reserved marinade, add brown sugar, vinegar, rosemary and bay leaf. Pour over beef mixture. Reduce heat. Simmer, covered, until beef is tender, about 1 hour. Discard bay leaf. Add olives. Simmer 5 minutes. Makes 4 servings.

Melon-Marmalade Medley

Cool and refreshing dessert—or serve as a fruit cocktail to start a meal.

1/2 cup orange marmalade
1/4 cup orange juice
2 teaspoons lemon juice
1 teaspoon finely chopped candied ginger
2 cups cantaloupe balls (1 melon)

3 cups honeydew melon balls
   (1 large melon)
2 cups watermelon balls,
   seeded (about 1/4 melon)

In a small bowl, combine marmalade, orange juice, lemon juice and ginger; set aside. In a large serving bowl, combine cantaloupe, honeydew and watermelon balls. Pour marmalade mixture over melon balls. Toss gently. Cover and refrigerate until ready to serve. Makes 8 servings.

Variation
Melon-Marmalade Salad: After chilling, drain juice from melon balls. Combine 3 tablespoons juice with 1-1/2 cups dairy sour cream. Arrange melon balls on lettuce leaves on individual serving plates. Top with sour-cream mixture. Garnish with fresh mint sprigs, if desired.

When using bay leaves, check the label. French bay leaves are mild, but those from California have a strong flavor. French bay leaves may remain in a dish throughout cooking, but California leaves should be removed after the dish has cooked 20 to 30 minutes.

Grandma Lauder's Crown Puddings

Hearty old-fashioned dessert with a heady—but strictly temperate—sauce.

1 cup strawberry or
   raspberry preserves or jam
2 cups all-purpose flour
1 tablespoon baking powder
1/4 teaspoon salt
1/2 cup butter or margarine,
   room temperature

1/2 cup sugar
2 egg whites, slightly beaten
1 teaspoon vanilla extract
3/4 cup milk
Granny's Eggnog Sauce, see below

Granny's Eggnog Sauce:
2 egg yolks
1/2 cup sifted powdered sugar
1/2 teaspoon rum extract

1/2 teaspoon brandy extract
1 cup whipping cream, whipped

Preheat oven to 350F (175C). Butter 8 custard cups. Spoon 2 tablespoons preserves or jam into bottom of each custard cup; set aside. In a medium bowl, combine flour, baking powder and salt. Stir with a slotted spoon to blend. In large bowl of electric mixer, cream butter or margarine and sugar until light. Add egg whites. Beat until blended. Stir vanilla into milk. Add flour mixture and milk mixture alternately to sugar mixture, beginning and ending with flour; beat well after each addition. Spoon into prepared cups. Bake in preheated oven until tops spring back when lightly touched with your finger, about 25 minutes. Prepare Granny's Eggnog Sauce. Invert puddings onto individual serving dishes. Serve hot or at room temperature. Pass sauce separately. Makes 8 servings.

Granny's Eggnog Sauce:
In a small bowl, beat egg yolks, sugar and extracts with electric mixer until mixture is pale. Fold into whipped cream. Makes about 2 cups. This sauce is also excellent to serve over fresh or canned fruit.

Whipped Cream That Behaves

Last-minute beating of cream for a party dessert is a nuisance. Here's the solution.

1/4 cup cold water
2 teaspoons unflavored gelatin
1 qt. whipping cream

1 cup sifted powdered sugar
2 teaspoons vanilla extract

Pour water into a medium saucepan. Sprinkle gelatin over surface of water. Let stand 3 to 4 minutes to soften. Stir over very low heat until gelatin dissolves. Cool 10 minutes. Gradually stir in cream. Pour into a medium bowl. Refrigerate at least 30 minutes or up to 4 hours. Set aside 1/3 cup cream mixture. With electric mixer, beat remaining cream until stiff. Beat in sugar and vanilla. Gently stir in reserved cream. Cover and refrigerate from 1 to 3 hours. Stir gently before serving. Makes about 2 quarts.

Variation
This stabilized whipped cream may be flavored with any extract desired instead of vanilla.

Swedish Limpa   Photo on page 41.

This is the justly famous rye bread with a delicate flavor of orange.

1 (1/4-oz.) pkg. active dry yeast
    (1 tablespoon)
2 cups warm water (110F, 45C)
1/4 cup packed dark-brown sugar
1 tablespoon molasses

1/4 cup vegetable shortening, melted
2 teaspoons grated orange peel
1 tablespoon salt
2-1/4 cups medium rye flour
3-1/2 cups all-purpose flour

In a 1-cup measure, stir yeast into 1/2 cup warm water. Add 1 tablespoon brown sugar. Stir until yeast is dissolved. Let stand until bubbly and doubled in volume, about 10 minutes. In a large bowl, combine remaining warm water and brown sugar with molasses, shortening, orange peel and salt. Stir to blend. Stir in yeast mixture. Add rye flour; beat well. Gradually stir in enough all-purpose flour to make a stiff dough. Turn out onto a lightly floured surface. Clean and grease bowl; set aside. Knead dough until smooth and elastic, about 8 minutes, adding enough of remaining all-purpose flour to keep dough from sticking. Place dough in greased bowl, turning to grease all sides. Cover with a dry cloth. Let rise in a warm place, free from drafts, until doubled in bulk, 1 to 1-1/2 hours. Grease 1 large or 2 medium baking sheets. Punch down dough. Knead 5 or 6 times. Divide dough in half. Shape each half into an oval loaf. Place on prepared baking sheet. Cover and let rise until doubled in bulk, about 40 minutes. Preheat oven to 350F (175C). With a thin, sharp knife, cut 1/2-inch-deep slashes across tops of loaves at 2-inch intervals. Bake until loaves are browned and sound hollow when tapped, about 50 minutes. Cool on wire racks. Makes 2 loaves.

Old-Fashioned Buckwheat Cakes

Unique flavor of buckwheat is enhanced with maple and cinnamon.

3/4 cup all-purpose flour
3/4 cup buckwheat flour
1/2 teaspoon salt
1/4 cup packed light-brown sugar
1 tablespoon baking powder
2 eggs, slightly beaten

1-1/4 cups milk
1/2 teaspoon maple extract
1/2 teaspoon butter-flavor extract
1/4 teaspoon cinnamon extract
1/4 cup vegetable oil
Shortening, butter or margarine for griddle

Preheat griddle as manufacturer directs. In a large bowl or wide-mouthed pitcher, combine flours, salt, brown sugar and baking powder. With a fork, stir until blended. In a small bowl, combine eggs, milk, extracts and oil. Beat to blend. Gradually stir into flour mixture, only until evenly moistened. Batter will be lumpy. Grease griddle lightly. Pour batter onto griddle to form pancakes, using about 3 tablespoons for each cake and allowing spreading space between them. Cook until bubbles form over surface. Turn and cook other side until browned. Keep warm while cooking remainder of cakes. Makes 16 to 18 pancakes.

How to Make Swedish Limpa

1/Knead dough until smooth and elastic.

2/Punch down risen dough.

3/Shape each half into an oval loaf.

4/Let rise until doubled. Slash tops of loaves.

Daria's Lime Teacake

This cake, light and delicate as a cloud, is good alone or with fruit or sherbet.

6 eggs
1-3/4 cups all-purpose flour
1/2 teaspoon salt
5 tablespoons fresh lime juice

1 tablespoon cold water
1-1/2 cups granulated sugar
1 tablespoon grated lime peel
Sifted powdered sugar

One hour before preparing cake, separate eggs, placing whites in a large bowl and yolks in small bowl of electric mixer. Let stand at room temperature. Sift flour. Measure and sift again with salt; set aside. In a small bowl, combine lime juice and water; set aside. At medium speed, beat egg whites until foamy. Gradually beat in 1/2 cup granulated sugar. Continue beating until stiff peaks form. Preheat oven to 350F (175C). Beat yolks until thick and pale, at least 5 minutes. Slowly add remaining 1 cup granulated sugar to yolks, beating until smooth. At low speed, beat in a fourth of the flour mixture, then a third of the lime juice mixture, until blended. Repeat with remaining flour and juice mixtures, ending with flour. Beat in lime peel. With a spatula or whisk, fold batter into beaten whites just until no streaks of white show. Pour into an ungreased 10-inch tube pan or Bundt pan. Bake in preheated oven until cake springs back when gently pressed with your fingertips, 35 to 40 minutes. Invert pan, placing neck of a funnel or a large bottle in tube. Let cake hang until completely cooled. Gently slide the blade of a thin knife around outer edge and tube edge to loosen cake from pan. Place a large plate over top of pan. Invert and shake cake to turn it out onto plate. Sprinkle with sifted powdered sugar. Makes 12 servings.

Big-Surprise Creams

Plain-looking candies that contain an amazing symphony of flavors.

4 cups sugar
1-1/2 cups cold water
1-1/2 tablespoons white vinegar
3 egg whites

2 teaspoons vanilla extract
2 teaspoons chocolate extract
1/2 teaspoon walnut or
    black walnut extract

In a medium saucepan, combine sugar, water and vinegar. Stir constantly over medium heat until sugar is dissolved. Attach a candy thermometer to side of pan, if desired. Bring liquid to a boil. Reduce heat so mixture boils slowly. Boil sugar syrup until it reaches 234F to 240F (111C to 118C) on thermometer. Or, boil to soft-ball stage—until 1/2 teaspoon syrup dropped into cold water can be shaped into a ball that flattens when removed from water. While candy cooks, generously butter a large baking sheet. In a large bowl, beat egg whites until soft peaks form. While constantly beating egg whites, slowly pour in cooked syrup. Add extracts. Beat until creamy. Drop from a teaspoon in mounds onto prepared baking sheet. Cool 15 minutes. To keep candies, cover them with a sheet of foil. Leave at room temperature up to 4 days. Makes 40 to 60 pieces.

Variations
Top each cream with one of the following: half a nut, half a candied cherry and a small piece of candied citron, a piece of candied orange peel, a small piece of milk chocolate, or a small piece of bittersweet chocolate.

Every-Which-Way Pound Cake

Unusual combination of extracts produces a wonderful what-is-it flavor.

1 cup butter or margarine, room temperature	1 teaspoon vanilla extract
1/2 cup vegetable shortening	1 teaspoon coconut extract
3 cups sugar	1/2 teaspoon rum extract
5 eggs, well beaten	1/2 teaspoon lemon extract
3 cups all-purpose flour	1/2 teaspoon pistachio extract
1/2 teaspoon baking powder	1/4 teaspoon almond extract
1 cup milk	Every-Which-Way Glaze, see below

Every-Which-Way Glaze:

1 cup sugar	1/4 teaspoon rum extract
1/2 cup water	1/2 teaspoon coconut extract
1/4 teaspoon lemon extract	1/4 teaspoon pistachio extract
1 teaspoon vanilla extract	3 drops almond extract

Preheat oven to 325F (165C). Grease and flour a 10-inch tube pan; set aside. In large bowl of electric mixer, beat butter or margarine, shortening and sugar at low speed until fluffy. At low speed, beat in eggs. Mix flour and baking powder. At medium speed, add to sugar mixture alternately with milk, beginning and ending with flour mixture. Add all flavoring extracts. Reduce speed to low and beat until combined. Spoon into prepared pan. Bake in preheated oven until a wooden pick inserted in center comes out clean, about 1-1/2 hours. Cool in pan on a rack, 10 minutes. While cake cools, prepare Every-Which-Way Glaze. Turn cake out onto a serving plate. With a thin skewer or cake tester, pierce cake all over almost to center. Slowly pour hot glaze over hot cake; glaze will be absorbed by cake. Cool 1-1/2 hours at room temperature before serving. Makes 16 to 18 servings.

Every-Which-Way Glaze:
In a heavy saucepan, combine all ingredients. Bring to a boil over medium-high heat, stirring constantly. Reduce heat to medium-low. Cook and stir until sugar is dissolved, about 5 minutes.

Citrus-Buttermilk Sherbet

Easy, tangy, mellowed-with-honey dessert to make ahead on a hot summer day.

1 qt. buttermilk	2 tablespoons lime juice
1/4 cup honey	1 teaspoon grated lemon peel
2 tablespoons lemon juice	1 teaspoon grated lime peel

In blender or food processor, process all ingredients until smooth. Pour into a 9-inch square baking pan. Cover. Place in freezer until firm around edge but soft in center, 1 to 2 hours. With a fork, beat mixture until smooth. Cover and return to freezer until firm, about 4 hours. Place in refrigerator 15 minutes before serving to soften slightly. Makes 6 servings.

How to Make Raspberry Rapture

1/Spread raspberry-juice mixture over trimmed cake. Roll up cake, using towel to help roll evenly.

2/Pipe whipped-cream mixture over top of roll. Decorate with reserved raspberries.

Atlantic City Macaroons

These chewy, crunchy cookies used to be sold—perhaps still are—on the resort's boardwalk.

1 (7- or 8-oz.) can or pkg. almond paste
2 egg whites
1/8 teaspoon salt

1/2 teaspoon vanilla extract
1/4 teaspoon almond extract
1 cup powdered sugar, sifted

Preheat oven to 325F (165C). Grease baking sheets. Dust lightly with flour, then tap off excess. In large bowl of electric mixer, break up almond paste. Add unbeaten egg whites, salt and extracts. With electric mixer at low speed, beat until mixture is smooth. Gradually add sugar, beating until a soft dough forms. Drop by scant teaspoons onto prepared baking sheets, about 1/2 inch apart. Dough spreads very little in baking. Bake in preheated oven until light golden brown, about 20 minutes. With a spatula, remove immediately to wire racks to cool. Macaroons can be stored 4 to 6 days in an airtight metal container at room temperature. They will become harder but are still good. Or, they can be wrapped airtight and frozen. Makes about 36 cookies.

Raspberry Rapture

Cousin to old-fashioned jelly roll.

1 (10-oz.) pkg. sweetened frozen
   raspberries, thawed
Raspberry-Juice Custard, see below
4 eggs, separated
1 cup granulated sugar
1-1/2 teaspoons raspberry extract

1 cup cake flour
1/2 teaspoon baking powder
2 tablespoons boiling water
Powdered sugar
1 cup whipping cream
2 tablespoons powdered sugar

Raspberry-Juice Custard:
Juice from raspberries, see above
Cold water
2 tablespoons cornstarch

1 egg, slightly beaten
1 teaspoon butter

Drain raspberries, reserving juice in a 1-cup measure. Refrigerate raspberries. Prepare Raspberry-Juice Custard. Preheat oven to 375F (190C). Grease a 15" x 10" baking sheet with raised sides. Line with waxed paper; set aside. In a large bowl, beat egg whites with electric mixer until stiff but not dry; set aside. In a small bowl, beat yolks until pale. Add granulated sugar and 1 teaspoon raspberry extract. Beat until thick and pale. Fold into egg whites. Sift together flour and baking powder, then sift over top of egg mixture. By hand, gently fold together. Fold in water. Spread mixture evenly in prepared pan. Bake in preheated oven until center springs back when lightly touched, about 8 minutes. Dampen a cloth towel with cold water. Wring very dry. Or, use a dry towel. Spread out on a flat surface. Sprinkle lightly with powdered sugar. Invert cake onto cloth. Remove waxed paper. With a sharp knife, cut off extreme edges of cake. Roll up cake and towel, beginning from a long side. Set aside 5 to 10 minutes. Whip cream. Divide in 2 equal parts. Fold 1 part into Raspberry-Juice Custard. Unroll cake and towel. Spread custard mixture over cake. Roll up cake and filling, using towel to help roll evenly. Place rolled cake on a platter. Sprinkle top of roll lightly with powdered sugar. Into remaining 1 cup whipped cream, fold remaining 1/2 teaspoon raspberry extract and 2 tablespoons powdered sugar. Pipe or spoon in a decorative line along top of roll. Top with reserved raspberries. Makes 8 to 10 servings.

Raspberry-Juice Custard:
To reserved raspberry juice in measure, add cold water to make 1 cup. Pour juice mixture into top of a double boiler. Stir cornstarch into juice mixture until dissolved. Stir in egg and butter. Stir over simmering water until thickened. Cool slightly; refrigerate.

Variations
Substitute frozen strawberries and strawberry extract for frozen raspberries and raspberry extract.

Substitute frozen peaches and 1 teaspoon nutmeg extract for frozen raspberries and raspberry extract.

For an unusual spread for bread or toast, stir 1 tablespoon snipped fresh marjoram leaves into 2 cups orange marmalade, or 4 teaspoons snipped fresh mint leaves into 2 cups peach or apricot preserves.

Gingery Orange-Chiffon Pie

An exceptional crust brings new distinction to an old favorite.

Gingery Pastry, see below
3/4 cup sugar
1 (.25-oz.) envelope unflavored gelatin
    (1 tablespoon)

1 cup orange juice
4 eggs, separated
1 tablespoon grated orange peel

Gingery Pastry:
1-1/4 cups all-purpose flour
2 tablespoons minced candied ginger
1/4 teaspoon ground cardamom

1/2 cup cold butter or margarine,
    cut into pieces
3 to 4 tablespoons cold orange juice

Prepare and bake Gingery Pastry. In top of a double boiler, combine 1/2 cup sugar, gelatin, orange juice and egg yolks. Stir to blend. Cook and stir over hot water until thickened. Stir in orange peel. Refrigerate until mixture forms small mounds when dropped from a spoon, 30 to 45 minutes. In a large bowl, beat egg whites until foamy. Slowly add remaining 1/4 cup sugar, beating until mixture is stiff. Gently fold egg-white mixture into orange mixture. Spoon into cooled pie shell. Refrigerate until set, about 4 hours. Just before serving, sprinkle with reserved pastry crumbs. Makes 6 to 8 servings.

Gingery Pastry:
In a medium bowl, combine flour, ginger and cardamom. With a pastry blender or two forks, cut in butter or margarine until fine crumbs form. Gradually stir in orange juice with a fork just until mixture comes away from side of bowl. Shape into a ball. Pinch off about one-fourth of dough and wrap in foil. Wrap remaining portion in foil. Refrigerate both portions 2 hours. Preheat oven to 425F (220C). On a lightly floured surface, roll larger piece of dough to an 11-inch circle. Ease into a 9-inch pie plate. Without stretching, press gently over bottom and side of pan. Trim edge even with pan. Prick dough all over with a fork. Line with foil. Fill foil with dried beans or rice. Roll remaining dough to 1/8-inch thickness. Place on an ungreased baking sheet. Prick all over with a fork. Bake shell and flattened dough in preheated oven 10 minutes. Remove foil and beans or rice from pastry in pie plate. Bake shell and flattened dough until golden, 8 to 10 minutes longer. Cool on a wire rack. Crumble flattened dough to make fine crumbs; set aside. Cover pastry and set aside at room temperature.

Coconut-Cornflake Cookies

These macaroon-chewy cookies are a favorite with kids, but adults won't say no.

4 egg whites, room temperature
1/2 teaspoon salt
1/2 teaspoon cream of tartar
1-1/4 cups sugar

1-1/4 teaspoons coconut-flavor extract
4 cups cornflakes
1 (3-1/2-oz.) pkg. grated coconut

Preheat oven to 300F (150C). Grease baking sheets; set aside. In large bowl of electric mixer, beat egg whites on medium speed until frothy. Add salt and cream of tartar. Beat to combine. Gradually add sugar, beating until egg whites are stiff. Beat in extract. By hand, gently fold in cornflakes and coconut. Drop by teaspoons onto prepared baking sheets. Bake in preheated oven until firm, about 20 minutes. Cookies can be stored up to 1 week in an airtight metal container at room temperature, or wrapped airtight and frozen. Makes about 84 cookies.

Summertime Coolers

Tall, refreshing fruit drinks to serve when the temperature climbs.

Peach Smoothie

3 fresh peaches, peeled, cut in chunks
2 cups orange juice

In blender, process peaches and orange juice until smooth. Pour into undivided freezer tray. Freeze until solid, 2 to 3 hours. Cut into chunks. Return to blender. Process just until soft enough to pour. Pour into drinking glasses. Serve immediately. Makes 4 to 6 servings.

Orange-Buttermilk Delight

1 qt. buttermilk
3/4 cup frozen orange-juice concentrate,
   thawed

Ice cubes
Mint sprigs

In blender, process buttermilk and orange concentrate until blended. Place ice cubes in 6 tall drinking glasses. Pour buttermilk mixture over ice cubes. Garnish with mint. Serve immediately. Makes 6 servings.

Chilly Lime Cream

2 cups plain yogurt
1/4 cup lime juice

2 tablespoons honey
1-1/2 cups crushed ice

In blender, process yogurt, lime juice and honey until blended. Add ice. Blend 15 seconds. Pour into drinking glasses. Serve immediately. Makes 4 servings.

Down-Home Pink Lemonade

1 cup water
2 cups superfine sugar
1-1/2 cups strained fresh lemon juice
1 cup cranberry juice

Ice cubes
Cold water
Thin lemon slices, if desired

In a medium saucepan, combine water and sugar. Stir over low heat until sugar is completely dissolved. Cool to room temperature. Stir in lemon juice. Pour mixture into a jar with a tight-fitting lid. Refrigerate. Shake to blend before serving. For each drink, pour 1/4 cup lemon mixture and 1 tablespoon cranberry juice over ice cubes in a tall drinking glass. Pour cold water into glass until full. Stir to blend. Garnish each glass with a lemon slice, if desired. Makes 16 servings.

Minted Orangeade

2-1/2 cups water
1-1/2 cups sugar
1 cup lightly crushed fresh mint leaves
1 teaspoon grated orange peel

2 cups orange juice
1-1/4 cups lemon juice
Ice cubes
Ginger-ale, chilled

In a medium saucepan, combine water and sugar. Bring to a boil, stirring over medium-high heat. Place mint leaves in a medium glass or pottery bowl. Pour hot sugar mixture over leaves. Add orange peel, orange juice and lemon juice. Cover and let stand 1-1/2 hours. Strain, reserving juice in a jar with a tight-fitting lid. Cover and refrigerate. For each serving, pour 1/3 cup strained juice mixture over ice cubes in a tall drinking glass. Pour ginger-ale into glass until full. Makes about 16 servings.

Pineberry Refresher

1 (6-oz.) can frozen pineapple-juice
   concentrate, thawed
1 (6-oz.) can frozen cranberry-juice
   concentrate, thawed

1 qt. cold water
Ice cubes
1 pint pineapple sherbet
Mint sprigs, if desired

Pour juice concentrates into a large bowl or pitcher. Add water, stirring to dissolve concentrates. Pour over ice cubes in tall drinking glasses. Top each serving with a small scoop of sherbet and a mint sprig, if desired. Makes 6 to 8 servings.

Coffee, Tea & Chocolate

In today's markets, we find coffees and teas—the common to the exotic—from all over the world. There are also coffees and teas with added spices, fruit peel and other flavorings.

Coffee is grown primarily in Central and South America. African, Mexican and Hawaiian coffees are also available. Among the well-known varieties, *mocha* from Yemen is strong and full-bodied, with a slight chocolate flavor; *kona* from Hawaii is delicate and light-bodied; *harar* from Ethiopia is full-bodied and has a rather tart flavor.

Tea is made from the leaves of the *camellia sinensis* shrub. China, India and Japan are the principal producers of tea for the world. There are basically three types of teas, all of which come from the same source. The differences are in the processing. Unfermented tea produces *green* tea; semi-fermented tea is *oolong;* fermented tea is *black* tea.

Caffeine-free herbal teas brewed from either fresh or dried herbs are a delightful alternative to coffee or tea. Experiment and discover the vast array of flavor combinations. Any of the mints are refreshing alone or in combination with other beverages. For delicate flavors try alfalfa, chamomile, catnip or comfrey. For more pronounced flavors use anise, caraway, dill or fennel seeds. Rosemary and sage can be combined with milder herbs or teas. Lemon flavor is available in plants other than citrus. Delicious tea, either hot or cold, can be made from lemon balm, lemon geranium, lemongrass, lemon thyme or lemon verbena.

Neither coffee nor tea is limited to use as a beverage. Coffee, particularly when paired with chocolate, gives rich flavor to cakes, cookies, frostings, puddings and ice creams. Scandinavians like to baste roasting lamb or veal with coffee. In the Caribbean and South America, coffee teams with fish in a number of dishes. Tea is not quite as versatile as a flavoring agent. A number of fruit punches and other drinks are based on tea, as well as a delicate Belgian sherbet and an excellent Danish quick bread.

Chocolate came to Europe from the New World, courtesy of the explorers. Hernando Cortez learned the secrets of using chocolate. Today we can buy bitter, semisweet and milk chocolate, in solid, powdered and syrup forms.

Menu

Come for Dessert & Coffee

Fruit & Cheese Tray
Assorted Crackers
Gingery-Orange Chiffon Pie, page 74
Raspberry Rapture, page 73
Café Brûlot, page 84
Viennese Snowtop Coffee, page 20
Honey-Nectarine Brandy, page 44

Ham With Coffee Glaze

Coffee tempers the sweetness of the glaze and contributes unusual flavor.

1 slice fully cooked ham,
   about 1-1/2 inches thick
1-1/2 teaspoons instant coffee powder
2 tablespoons orange juice

1/4 cup dark corn syrup
1/4 cup packed light-brown sugar
1 tablespoon butter or margarine

Preheat oven to 325F (165C). Place ham in a shallow baking dish. Cover and bake 30 minutes. While ham bakes, in a small saucepan combine coffee and orange juice; stir to blend. Add syrup, sugar and butter or margarine. Stir over low heat, until combined and heated through. Spoon coffee mixture over ham. Bake, uncovered, 30 minutes longer, basting occasionally with pan juices. Serve immediately. Makes 4 servings.

Oriental Tea-Smoked Chicken

Delicately fragrant, exotic in flavor, this is chicken very much out of the ordinary.

1 tablespoon coarsely ground black pepper
2 tablespoons salt
1 (4-lb.) roasting chicken

1 tablespoon black tea leaves
1 tablespoon uncooked rice
1 tablespoon brown sugar

One day before serving, combine pepper and salt. Rub over skin and into cavity of chicken. Wrap tightly in foil and refrigerate overnight. With a damp towel or cloth, gently wipe chicken inside and out, to remove most of pepper mixture. Pour water to a depth of about 2 inches into bottom of a wok or steamer. Position rack over water. Place chicken on rack. Bring water to a boil. Reduce heat. Cover tightly and steam 45 minutes. Drain chicken well. Let stand at room temperature until cool and dry. Line bottom of a large pot with foil. Combine tea, rice and sugar. Spread over foil. Position a small rack over foil. Place chicken on rack, breast side up. Cover tightly. Place over medium heat. When tea leaves make a crackling noise, start timing chicken to smoke 5 minutes. Turn off heat; let stand 5 minutes. Remove cover. If chicken is not well-browned, replace cover and smoke over medium heat an additional 3 to 4 minutes. Serve hot or cold. Makes 4 to 6 servings.

Hawaiian Frosty

Unusual combination of flavors in a smooth, rich beverage.

2 cups strong brewed coffee, chilled
1 cup pineapple juice, chilled

1 pint vanilla ice cream, softened
Ice cubes

In a large bowl, combine coffee, pineapple juice and ice cream. Beat with electric mixer at low speed until smooth. Pour over ice cubes in tall drinking glasses. Makes 4 servings.

Chinese Tea Eggs

Appetizer or snack with an intriguing flavor and handsome, marbleized appearance.

10 eggs
Water
3 tea bags

1/3 cup light soy sauce
1 teaspoon anise seeds

Place eggs in a 2-quart saucepan. Add water to cover. Bring to a boil. Reduce heat. Simmer, covered, 10 minutes. Remove eggs, reserving water. Cool eggs in cold water. With the back of a teaspoon, crack eggshells gently all over. Do not remove shells. Return to reserved water. Bring to a boil. Add tea bags, soy sauce and anise seeds. Reduce heat. Simmer, covered, 1 hour. Store covered, in cold water, in refrigerator up to 5 days. Change water daily. Peel to serve. Makes 10 servings.

Panned Steaks Brazilian-Style

How can such a little extra flavoring make such a big difference?

4 (1-inch) boneless rib-eye steaks
About 1 tablespoon vegetable oil
1/4 cup butter or margarine
1/4 teaspoon garlic juice

1 cup strong brewed coffee
Salt and ground black pepper
1/2 cup thinly sliced green onions
   with some tops

Slash edges of steaks to prevent curling during cooking. Place a large, heavy skillet over high heat. When it is hot, cover bottom with a very thin film of oil. Add steaks. Cook 1 minute on each side. Reduce heat to medium-high. Continue to cook and turn steaks 2 more minutes on each side for rare, 3 minutes for medium, 3-1/2 minutes for medium-well done, 4 to 5 minutes for well done. Remove steaks to a heated platter; keep warm. Place butter or margarine and garlic juice in skillet. Reduce heat to medium. When butter or margarine melts, add coffee. Stir to combine, scraping bottom of skillet to loosen browned steak juices. Cook over high heat until reduced by about half. Season to taste with salt and pepper. Pour sauce over steaks. Sprinkle green onions over steaks. Serve immediately. Makes 4 servings.

Because homemade bread contains no preservatives, it goes stale fast. Don't let it go to waste—make croutons with homemade herb bread. Cut into cubes; bake in a slow oven until dry. Drizzle with melted butter or margarine. Toss lightly to coat; bake again until crisp. Store in an airtight container.

How to Make Chinese Tea Eggs

1/With the back of a teaspoon, gently crack cooked eggs all over; do not remove shells.

2/After further cooking in tea mixture, refrigerate until served. Remove shells to serve.

Sole Caribbean

Bathed in a coffee-lemon marinade, fish takes on great new flavor.

2 lbs. fresh sole fillets	1/2 teaspoon salt
4 teaspoons instant coffee powder	1 teaspoon onion powder
2 tablespoons lemon juice	Thin lemon slices, if desired
6 tablespoons vegetable oil	

Place fish in a single layer in a large shallow dish. Mix instant coffee with lemon juice until dissolved. Stir in oil, salt and onion powder until blended. Pour coffee mixture over fish; let stand 15 minutes. Turn fish; let stand 15 minutes longer. Preheat broiler, if manufacturer directs. Broil fish 3 inches from heat until fish flakes easily when pierced with a fork, 5 to 7 minutes. Garnish with lemon slices, if desired. Makes 4 to 6 servings.

Variations
Substitute fresh flounder or frozen sole or flounder fillets, thawed, for the fresh sole.

Heavenly Devil's Food

This is the best of all chocolate cakes—moist, light, richly satisfying.

Cocoa Base, see below
3/4 cup butter or margarine,
  room temperature
1 cup sugar
2 eggs, well beaten
2 teaspoons vanilla extract

2 cups cake flour
1 teaspoon baking soda
1/8 teaspoon salt
1/2 cup milk
Fudge Frosting, see below

Cocoa Base:
1 cup sugar
3/4 cup unsweetened cocoa powder

1 egg, well-beaten
1 cup milk

Fudge Frosting:
3 (6-oz.) pkgs. semisweet real
  chocolate pieces
9 tablespoons butter or margarine
1-1/2 teaspoons instant coffee powder

3/4 cup hot water
5-1/2 cups powdered sugar, sifted
1/4 teaspoon salt
1 tablespoon vanilla extract

Prepare Cocoa Base. Preheat oven to 375F (190C). Generously butter 2 round 9-inch or 3 round 8-inch cake pans. In a large bowl, cream butter or margarine and sugar until light and fluffy. Add eggs; beat well. Beat in vanilla. Sift flour before measuring, then sift again with baking soda and salt. Alternately add flour mixture and milk to sugar mixture, beating well after each addition. Beat in cooled Cocoa Base. Pour into prepared pans. Bake in preheated oven until cake shrinks slightly from sides of pans and springs back when touched lightly with your fingertips, about 25 minutes for 8-inch or 20 minutes for 9-inch layers. Cool 10 minutes in pans. Turn out onto wire racks to cool completely. Prepare Fudge Frosting. Spread between layers and over top and sides. Makes about 12 servings.

Cocoa Base:
In top of a double boiler, combine sugar and cocoa. Stir in egg, then milk, until combined. Stirring frequently, cook over hot, not boiling, water until thick and smooth, 10 to 15 minutes. Cool completely before using.

Fudge Frosting:
In top of a double boiler over hot, not boiling water, melt chocolate and butter or margarine. Remove from heat. Dissolve instant coffee in hot water. Alternately add coffee mixture and sugar to chocolate mixture, stirring to blend after each addition. Stir in salt and vanilla. Beat until thick enough to spread. Makes enough to fill three 8- or two 9-inch layers, and to frost tops and sides.

Chocolate burns easily. Melt it in the top of a double boiler over simmering water, or in a small, heavy saucepan over lowest possible heat. Or, place chocolate pieces in a custard cup and set the cup in a saucepan of simmering water over low heat. Or, place the custard cup in the oven as it is preheated. Chocolate will melt in 3 to 4 minutes.

Elegant Mocha-Almond Ice Cream

One of the best homemade frozen desserts—an exotic flavor and sinfully rich.

6 egg yolks
1-1/2 cups sugar
1 qt. (4 cups) whipping cream
2 tablespoons vanilla extract
2 (1-oz.) squares semisweet chocolate

1/2 cup brewed espresso coffee,
 room temperature
1/4 cup coarsely ground roasted almonds
2 tablespoons coarsely ground
 Italian-roast coffee beans

In a large bowl, beat egg yolks with electric mixer until light. Beat in sugar until mixture is thick and pale. At lowest speed, beat in cream and vanilla until blended. Pour mixture into ice-cream canister; freeze in ice-cream maker as manufacturer directs until partially set. Melt chocolate in top of a double boiler over hot, not boiling, water. Cool. Remove dasher from partially set ice cream. Add cooled chocolate; blend thoroughly. Stir in coffee, almonds and ground coffee beans. Return dasher to ice-cream canister; freeze 20 minutes or until firm. Spoon into a mold or serving bowl. Cover and store in freezer until ready to serve. Makes 6 to 8 servings.

Hasty Mocha Sundaes

With ice cream in the freezer, you can serve this delicious dessert in no time.

Hasty Mocha Sauce, see below
1 pint vanilla ice cream
1 pint caramel or butterscotch ice cream

3/4 cup toasted slivered almonds,
 if desired

Prepare Hasty Mocha Sauce. Into each of 6 individual serving dishes, place alternating spoonfuls of vanilla and caramel or butterscotch ice cream. Top with warm sauce. Sprinkle each serving with 2 tablespoons almonds, if desired. Makes 6 servings.

Hasty Mocha Sauce

Easy-do topping for almost any flavor ice cream or plain cake.

1 (12-oz.) pkg. semisweet real
 chocolate pieces
1 teaspoon vanilla extract

1 tablespoon instant coffee powder
1/3 cup boiling water

In blender, combine chocolate and vanilla. Dissolve coffee powder in boiling water; immediately pour into blender. Process at medium speed until chocolate melts and mixture is smooth. Makes about 1-1/4 cups.

Mocha Mousse In No Time

Make this delightful, easy-do dessert in the morning with coffee from breakfast.

1 (6-oz.) pkg. semisweet real
  chocolate pieces
2 eggs
2 tablespoons rum or brandy,
  or 1 teaspoon vanilla extract

3 tablespoons hot strong brewed coffee
3/4 cup milk, scalded
Whipped cream, if desired

In blender, place chocolate and eggs. Add rum, brandy or vanilla. Process briefly. With blender on, slowly pour coffee and scalded milk through hole in blender cover. Cover and process at medium speed 2 minutes. Pour into 4 individual dessert dishes. Refrigerate at least 4 hours. Top each serving with whipped cream, if desired. Makes 4 servings.

Variation
Substitute 5 tablespoons orange juice for rum, brandy or vanilla extract.

Ultimate Fudge Sundae

Magically, the hot sauce turns into a crackling jacket for the gussied-up ice cream.

1-1/2 cups sugar
1 qt. vanilla ice cream, softened

1/2 cup chopped pecans, if desired
Ultimate Fudge Sauce, see below

Ultimate Fudge Sauce:
4 (1-oz.) squares unsweetened chocolate
2 tablespoons butter
2/3 cup boiling water

2 cups sugar
1/4 cup corn syrup
1 teaspoon vanilla extract

Butter a jelly-roll pan or large platter; set aside. Place sugar in a heavy skillet over low heat. Cook, stirring with a wooden spoon, until sugar melts and turns golden brown. Pour immediately in a thin layer into prepared pan or platter. Cool. Refrigerate until cold and brittle. Break into pieces into blender or food processor. Process until coarsely chopped. Fold into ice cream, along with pecans, if desired. Return ice cream to freezer to harden. Prepare Ultimate Fudge Sauce. To serve, divide ice cream among 6 serving dishes. Pour 3 generous tablespoons hot Ultimate Fudge Sauce over each. Serve immediately. Makes 6 servings.

Ultimate Fudge Sauce:
In a heavy saucepan, melt chocolate with butter over very low heat. Stir to blend. Add boiling water, then sugar and corn syrup, stirring to blend after each addition. Bring to a boil. Cover pan; boil, without stirring, 3 minutes. Remove cover; reduce heat. Boil slowly 5 minutes without stirring. Add vanilla. Serve immediately, or reheat in a double boiler before serving. Store leftover sauce, covered, in refrigerator. Makes about 2 cups.

Variations
Substitute chocolate or coffee ice cream for vanilla ice cream. Substitute salted peanuts for pecans.

South-of-the-Border Mocha

Rich, satisfying and fragrant; both a pick-me-up and a relaxer.

1 (1-oz.) square unsweetened chocolate
1/4 cup sugar
1/8 teaspoon salt
1 cup boiling water
1/2 cup milk

1/2 cup whipping cream
1-1/2 cups hot strong freshly brewed coffee
1 teaspoon vanilla extract
Cinnamon

In top of a double boiler over hot, not boiling water, melt chocolate. Add sugar, salt and water; stir well. Continue to heat 5 minutes. Pour milk and cream into a small saucepan. Place over low heat until mixture reaches boiling point; do not boil. Stir milk mixture and coffee into chocolate mixture. Beat well with a whisk. Stir in vanilla. Pour into mugs. Lightly sprinkle each serving with cinnamon. Serve immediately. Makes 4 servings.

Oriental Lemonade

Everyone's favorite summer refresher, with tea added for extra zip.

2 qts. cold water
5 tablespoons orange pekoe tea leaves
3/4 cup sugar

3/4 cup boiling water
3/4 cup lemon juice
Ice cubes

Bring cold water to a full, rolling boil over high heat. Place tea in a glass or earthenware pitcher. Pour water over tea. Let stand 4 minutes, then stir and strain. Return strained tea to pitcher. In a small saucepan, combine sugar and boiling water. Bring to a boil, stirring frequently. Reduce heat. Boil slowly 10 minutes. Add to tea. Stir in lemon juice. Stir to combine. Pour over ice cubes in tall drinking glasses. Makes 8 servings.

Café Brûlot

This after-dinner coffee spectacular is the perfect ending for a very special meal.

1 (3-inch) cinnamon stick
10 whole cloves
1 teaspoon grated orange peel
1/2 teaspoon grated lemon peel

12 sugar cubes
1 cup brandy
1/4 cup instant coffee powder
1 qt. boiling water

Break cinnamon stick into 4 pieces. Place in chafing dish with cloves, orange peel, lemon peel and sugar. Add brandy. Place over chafing dish flame. In another container, dissolve coffee powder in boiling water. When brandy mixture is warm, carefully ignite. Let burn 1 minute. Pour coffee mixture over flaming brandy. Stir well. Ladle into demitasse cups. Serve immediately. Makes 8 servings.

Wines & Spirits

Like the genie, bottles of spirits contain magic properties: delightful flavors that enhance and compliment the flavors of food.

There are a few simple rules that govern cooking with spirits. First, don't put into food anything that you would not enjoy drinking. Good wine or beer will work wonders in the kitchen.

Cooking with wine will make you neither drunk nor fat. At 172F (75C)—well below the boiling point—alcohol begins to evaporate. As the alcohol goes, so do most of the calories, leaving only mellow flavor behind. The later in the recipe you add wine or other spirits, the more intense the flavor will be.

All of the spirits—beer, liquor and wine—are natural tenderizers. Marinades made with spirits enrich the flavor of meat or poultry, and help break down coarse fibers.

A little dab of jam, jelly or marmalade, plus a couple of tablespoons of brandy, make a fine glaze for ham. Beer in batters makes them both light and flavorful. Wine in sauces—red wines for hearty foods, white wines for delicate ones—lends flavor as nothing else can. Liqueurs can serve as instant sauces for ices, ice creams and plain cakes.

Fruit cordials can be made at home, using fresh fruit, sugar and neutral spirits—vodka, rum or brandy are preferred. You'll find recipes for several of these in this section. You'll also find directions for making Rumtopf, an old-fashioned way of preserving the summer fruits for the cold months ahead. Used as a sauce, as a condiment, and in cooking, Rumtopf is stunningly delicious.

Your cooking repertoire will be enriched and your family and friends well pleased when you add these "spirited" recipes to your menus.

Menu

Football Season Tailgate Spread

Foot-of-the-Mountain Snack Cheese, page 58
Rye Crackers
Dippers & Snacks with Tapenade, page 100
Tipsy Turnovers, page 93
Beer-Batter Drumsticks, page 90
York State Apple Ketchup, page 157
Midsummer Chutney, page 145
Mediterranean Carrot Salad, page 15
Inebriated Watermelon, page 94
Hot Coffee & Iced Fruit Punch

Zarzuela de Pescados

Spanish main-dish seafood stew, cousin of French bouillabaisse and Italian cioppino.

16 mussels, in shell
12 small clams, in shell
1 cup all-purpose flour
Cold water
1/4 cup olive oil
2 large onions, chopped
2 garlic cloves, minced
1 red bell pepper, chopped
1 green bell pepper, chopped
1 (28-oz.) can plum tomatoes, undrained
1/4 teaspoon baking soda
1/4 cup Madeira wine
1/2 cup ground blanched almonds
1/4 teaspoon crushed saffron threads

1 teaspoon sugar
1 teaspoon salt
1/4 teaspoon coarsely ground black pepper
1 bay leaf
Red Garlic Sauce, see below
2 cups water
1-3/4 cups dry white wine or vermouth
1 tablespoon lemon juice
16 large deveined unshelled raw shrimp
Cold water
1/2 lb. sea scallops, rinsed, halved
1-1/2 lbs. cooked lobster or lobster tails,
    cut in large pieces
10 cooked king crab legs

Red Garlic Sauce:
6 garlic cloves, peeled
3 egg yolks
1/4 teaspoon salt
1/4 teaspoon red (cayenne) pepper

1/2 teaspoon sweet paprika
3/4 cup olive oil
1/3 cup hot broth from the stew

One day before serving, scrub mussels and clams, removing all beards and barnacles. Place in a large container. Add flour. Add cold water to cover. Let stand overnight. In a large pot, heat oil. Add onions, garlic and peppers. Cook over medium heat, stirring frequently, 5 minutes. Halve tomatoes lengthwise. Remove as many seeds as possible. With a fork, mash tomatoes lightly. Add tomatoes and their liquid to pot. Add baking soda, then Madeira. Bring to a boil. Add almonds, saffron, sugar, salt, pepper and bay leaf. Reduce heat. Cook, uncovered, until mixture is slightly reduced and thickened, about 30 minutes. Begin preparation of Red Garlic Sauce, but do not add broth. Set sauce aside. Gently stir water, wine or vermouth and lemon juice into pot. Simmer 10 minutes. Discard bay leaf. Add shrimp; simmer 5 minutes. Drain mussels and clams. Rinse well under cold running water. Place in a large saucepan. Add cold water to cover. Bring to a boil. Cover pan and cook until shells open, 2 to 3 minutes. If any shells remain closed, remove and discard. Add mussels and clams to pot. Strain liquid in which they were cooked through triple layers of cheesecloth. Add strained cooking liquid to pot. Add scallops; simmer 3 minutes. Add lobster meat and crab legs. Heat just to warm through, about 2 minutes. Finish preparation of Red Garlic Sauce by stirring in hot broth. To serve, ladle stew into bowls, making sure each bowl contains some of each kind of shellfish with the broth. Pass Red Garlic Sauce separately. Each person adds the amount desired to season the dish. Makes 8 to 10 servings.

Red Garlic Sauce:
Place garlic in small bowl of electric mixer. Crush garlic with pestle or back of a spoon. Add egg yolks, salt, red pepper and paprika. Beat at low speed until well blended. At medium speed, gradually add oil, beating constantly until sauce is the consistency of mayonnaise. By hand, gradually stir in hot broth. Makes about 1-1/2 cups.

Zarzuela de Pescados with Old-Country Breadsticks, page 36.

Greek Lamb Stew

Crusty bread, a tossed salad and oil-cured olives are perfect accompaniments.

1 tablespoon vegetable oil
2 lbs. boneless lamb shoulder,
 trimmed of fat, cut in 1-inch cubes
1-1/2 lbs. small white onions, peeled
1-1/2 cups dry red wine
3 tablespoons tomato paste
3 tablespoons red-wine vinegar
1 tablespoon packed dark-brown sugar

2 garlic cloves, minced
1 bay leaf
3 whole cloves
1 (4-inch) cinnamon stick
1 teaspoon salt
1/2 teaspoon ground cumin
1/4 teaspoon ground pepper

In a 6-quart Dutch oven, heat oil over medium heat. Add about half the lamb. Stirring occasionally, sauté until browned, 5 to 7 minutes. Remove with a slotted spoon. Add remaining meat. Sauté until browned. Remove with slotted spoon. Drain off fat. Return meat to pot. At root end of each onion, cut a small cross. Add onions and remaining ingredients to pot. Bring to a boil. Reduce heat. Simmer, covered, until meat is tender, about 1 hour. Discard bay leaf, cloves and cinnamon stick. Serve immediately; or cool slightly, refrigerate, and reheat before serving. Can also be spooned into container with airtight lid and frozen. Makes 6 to 8 servings.

Beer & Cheddar Soup

A soup-lover's delight, hearty yet subtly flavored; serve with toasted French bread.

2-1/2 cups beer (about 20 oz.)
2-1/2 tablespoons instant chicken-flavor
 bouillon powder or granules
1 cup shredded carrot
1 cup thinly sliced celery
2/3 cup thinly sliced onion

1/3 cup all-purpose flour
3 cups milk
4 cups shredded sharp Cheddar cheese (1 lb.)
1 teaspoon salt
1/4 teaspoon ground black pepper

In a 3-quart saucepan, combine beer and bouillon powder or granules. Cook over medium heat, stirring frequently, until dissolved. Add carrot and celery. Separate onion into rings; add to beer mixture. Bring to a boil. Reduce heat. Simmer, covered, 10 minutes. Place flour in small bowl. Gradually stir or whisk in 1-1/2 cups milk until smooth. Gradually stir into soup until blended. Stir remaining 1-1/2 cups milk into soup. Cook, stirring frequently, until thickened, about 15 minutes. Add cheese a little at a time, stirring after each addition, until cheese melts. Add salt and pepper. Cook 1 minute; do not boil. Serve immediately. Makes 6 to 8 servings.

To devein unshelled shrimp, slit shell down the back of the shrimp, using the point of a thin, sharp knife. Remove vein with point of knife or with a shrimp deveiner. The shell will remain attached.

Cumberland Ham

Beer, rosemary and onions give this pork roast superb flavor.

1 (8- to 12-lb.) fresh leg of pork (ham)
2 cups dark beer
1 large onion, sliced
1/2 cup all-purpose flour
1 teaspoon dried rubbed sage

1/2 teaspoon dried leaf rosemary
1 teaspoon salt
1 teaspoon brown sugar
1/4 teaspoon ground black pepper
Cumberland Sauce, page 102

Remove fresh ham from refrigerator 45 minutes before cooking. At the same time, in a small bowl, combine beer and onion. In a second small bowl, combine flour, sage, rosemary, salt, sugar and pepper. Preheat oven to 450F (230C). Wipe ham with a damp cloth. Rub flour mixture on all sides of ham. Place fat-side up on a rack in a shallow roasting pan. Insert meat thermometer in thickest part of ham, not touching bone. Place in preheated oven. Immediately reduce oven temperature to 325F (165C). Roast, uncovered, 30 minutes. Remove onion from beer; discard onion. Quickly baste ham with about 1/2 cup beer. Reserve remaining beer. Continue to roast until meat reaches an internal temperature of 175F (80C) on meat thermometer, about 30 minutes per pound. Baste meat with more reserved beer every 30 minutes. Remove ham from oven. Let stand 20 minutes before serving. Prepare Cumberland Sauce. Pass sauce separately. Makes 8 to 10 servings.

Ginger-Sherried Shrimp

Two old favorites get together in a delicate, delightfully flavored sauce.

1 large cucumber
1 teaspoon salt
Hot water
1/2 cup butter or margarine
2 green onions, with some tops, minced
2 tablespoons minced celery
1/4 cup all-purpose flour
1/8 teaspoon ground white pepper

1 cup milk
3/4 cup whipping cream
1/4 cup sherry from Sherry-Preserved Ginger,
   page 96
3/4 lb. deveined shelled cooked shrimp
4 slices firm white bread,
   toasted, crusts removed
Paprika

With a fork, score peel of cucumber from top to bottom. Cut in half lengthwise. Use a teaspoon to remove seeds. Cut crosswise into 1/4-inch slices. In medium saucepan, combine cucumber slices, 1/2 teaspoon salt and hot water to cover. Cook over medium heat until cucumber is crisp-tender, about 7 minutes. Drain well; set aside. In a medium saucepan, melt butter or margarine over low heat. Add green onions and celery. Cook until tender, 3 to 4 minutes. Stir in flour, pepper, and remaining 1/2 teaspoon salt. Stir vigorously until mixture forms a paste. Gradually stir in milk, then cream. Cook, stirring constantly, until mixture bubbles and thickens. Stir in sherry. Add cooked cucumber and shrimp. Heat through, but do not boil. Cut toast slices in half crosswise to form triangles. Place 2 toast triangles on each of 4 individual serving plates. Spoon shrimp, cucumber and sauce over toast. Sprinkle with paprika. Serve immediately. Makes 4 servings.

Beer-Batter Drumsticks

Succulent deep-fried chicken, with a savory coating of mustard and caraway batter.

1 cup all-purpose flour	**1 cup beer**
1 teaspoon caraway seeds	**8 chicken drumsticks**
1/4 teaspoon ground black pepper	**2 tablespoons sharp brown prepared mustard**
Salt	**Vegetable oil for deep-frying**

In a medium bowl, combine flour, caraway seeds, pepper and 1 teaspoon salt; stir to blend. Using a whisk, stir in beer until mixture is smooth. Let stand at room temperature 15 minutes to 1 hour. Sprinkle drumsticks lightly with salt, then brush with mustard. In a Dutch oven or deep-fat fryer, heat oil to 375F (190C). Heat oven to 200F (95C). One at a time, dip drumsticks in batter, coating on all sides. Let excess batter drip back into bowl. Fry a few at a time, so they will not be crowded, until golden brown and cooked through, 20 to 25 minutes. Drain on paper towels. Place fried drumsticks on a heated platter in oven to keep warm while frying remaining drumsticks. Makes 4 servings.

Variations
Use this beer batter when deep-frying other foods such as shrimp, pieces of fish fillet or chicken breast, flowerets of cauliflower or broccoli, parsley sprigs, asparagus tips and small whole mushrooms. If desired, serve with Oriental Sauces, page 107.

New Bedford Pot Roast

Serve noodles or rice and assorted relishes with this hearty rum-braised beef for a great meal.

1 (3- to 4-lb.) beef roast	**8 whole allspice**
1 teaspoon salt	**1 bay leaf, crumbled**
1/2 cup all-purpose flour	**1/2 cup golden or dark rum**
1/4 cup butter or margarine	**1/2 cup water**
2 garlic cloves, minced	**12 small whole carrots, scraped**
1 large onion, sliced	**1/2 cup snipped fresh dill**
12 black peppercorns	

Trim any excess fat from roast. Wipe roast with a damp cloth. Combine salt and flour. Rub well into meat on all sides. In a 6-quart Dutch oven, melt butter or margarine over low heat. Add garlic. Cook 2 minutes. Increase heat to medium. Add meat; brown well on all sides. Remove meat. Separate onion into rings. Place in a layer in bottom of Dutch oven. Return meat to pan. Add peppercorns, allspice and bay leaf. Pour rum over meat. Cover tightly. Reduce heat. Simmer very gently 3 to 4 hours, until meat is tender. At intervals during cooking time, add a little of the water until it is all used. When meat is nearly done, add carrots. Continue to simmer, covered, until meat and carrots are tender. Transfer meat to a heated platter. Place carrots around meat. Stir cooking liquid; taste and add more salt if required. Strain over roast and carrots. Sprinkle with dill. Makes 6 to 8 servings.

How to Make Beer-Batter Drumsticks

1/Spoon or brush mustard over chicken pieces, turning to coat all sides.

2/Dip coated drumsticks in batter, covering all sides. Let excess drip back into bowl.

Daria's Rum Cappuccino

A rich and heady hot beverage based on the Italian specialty.

3 cups strong freshly brewed coffee
3 cups half and half
1/2 cup crème de cacao liqueur

3/4 cup light rum
Sugar, if desired

In a medium saucepan, combine coffee, half and half, liqueur and rum. Place over medium heat until very hot. Do not boil. Pour into a jug or coffee pot and serve immediately. Let each person sweeten drink with sugar, if desired. Makes 6 to 8 servings.

Variation
Substitute brandy for rum, or use half rum and half brandy.

Roast Veal San Francisco-Style   Photo on page 146.

Serve to guests with curry-seasoned rice, page 131, self-sauced broccoli and a green salad.

1 (about 5-lb.) boned veal shoulder
  or rump roast
1 teaspoon dried leaf rosemary, crumbled
1/2 teaspoon dried leaf marjoram,
  crumbled
1/2 teaspoon garlic powder
1/2 teaspoon grated lemon peel
2 cups dry white wine
2 tablespoons vegetable oil

2 tablespoons butter or margarine
1/2 cup coarsely chopped walnuts
6 chicken livers
1/4 lb. mushrooms, coarsely chopped
1-1/2 cups hot water
1 tablespoon cornstarch
2 tablespoons cold water
1/2 teaspoon salt
1/4 teaspoon finely ground black pepper

One day before serving, wipe meat with a damp cloth and place in a large bowl. Combine rosemary, marjoram, garlic powder and lemon peel with 1/4 cup wine. When blended, stir in remaining wine and oil. Pour over roast. Cover and refrigerate overnight, turning several times. Preheat oven to 325F (165C). Place roast on a rack in a shallow pan; reserve marinade. Roast veal, uncovered, 35 minutes per pound or a total of about 3 hours. Baste frequently with some of reserved marinade. While roast cooks, melt butter or margarine in a medium skillet. Add walnuts; stir over medium heat until toasted. Remove with a slotted spoon; set aside. In same skillet, cook livers just until no longer red in center. Remove with a slotted spoon; set aside. Add more butter or margarine to skillet if necessary. Add mushrooms; cook 5 minutes. Chop livers coarsely. In same skillet, combine nuts, livers, mushrooms and 1/2 cup reserved marinade. Bring to a boil. Reduce heat and simmer 5 minutes. Remove roast to a heated platter. Skim off excess fat from drippings in roasting pan. Add hot water to roast drippings. Cook over medium heat, stirring constantly until drippings are dissolved. Stir in nut mixture. Mix cornstarch with cold water until smooth. Stir into gravy. Cook, stirring gently, until thickened and bubbling. Add salt and pepper. Slice roast. Spoon gravy over slices and serve immediately. Makes 6 to 8 servings.

Variation
Heat 1/4 cup Memorable Rosemary Jelly, page 147. Brush hot jelly over roasted veal on platter before carving. Garnish with fresh rosemary. Serve gravy separately.

Zabaglione

Serve hot or cooled, as is or as a sauce for fruit or plain cake.

6 egg yolks
2/3 cup superfine sugar

1/8 teaspoon salt
2/3 cup Marsala wine

In top of a double boiler, beat egg yolks until thick and pale. Add sugar a little at a time, beating well after each addition. Beat in salt and Marsala. Set over simmering, not boiling, water that does not touch bottom of pan. Beat constantly with a whisk until mixture is thick and foamy, 5 to 7 minutes. Turn off heat. Continue to beat 3 minutes. Serve immediately, or remove from hot water and cool, beating frequently. Makes 6 servings.

Tipsy Turnovers

Serve these spicy Norwegian meat pies for brunch, or take them on a picnic.

Tipsy Yogurt Sauce, see below
1 (11-oz.) pkg. pie-crust mix
1/4 cup brandy
1 tablespoon butter or margarine
2 large onions, finely chopped
4 eggs
2-1/2 teaspoons salt
1-1/2 teaspoons dry mustard
3/4 teaspoon ground allspice

3/4 teaspoon ground coriander
1/2 teaspoon black ground pepper
1/4 teaspoon ground cloves
2 lbs. lean ground pork
1 lb. lean ground beef
1-1/2 cups shredded Jarlsberg cheese
   (6 oz.)
1/4 cup roasted shelled sunflower seeds
1 tablespoon cold water

Tipsy Yogurt Sauce:
1 cup plain yogurt
1 cup dairy sour cream
1 tablespoon brandy

1 teaspoon grated lemon peel
2 tablespoons snipped fresh parsley

Prepare Tipsy Yogurt Sauce. Refrigerate until serving time. Prepare pie-crust mix according to package directions, using 1 tablespoon brandy as part of the liquid. Divide dough in half. Wrap each half in foil; refrigerate. In a large skillet, heat butter or margarine. Stir in onions. Cook until soft but not browned. Remove from heat. Add remaining 3 tablespoons brandy. Cool to room temperature. In a large bowl, beat 3 eggs until yolks and whites are combined. Beat in salt, mustard, allspice, coriander, pepper and cloves. Stir in onion mixture. Add meats, cheese and sunflower seeds. Stir gently until mixture is combined. On a lightly floured surface, roll out half of prepared pie-crust mix to a 12-inch circle. Transfer to a large baking sheet. Repeat with second half of dough, using a second baking sheet. Spoon half of meat mixture onto half of each dough circle. Fold second half of each circle over meat mixture. Press edges with tines of a fork to seal. Refrigerate 20 minutes. Preheat oven to 425F (220C). Beat remaining egg with cold water. Brush top of each turnover with egg mixture. Bake in preheated oven 20 minutes. Reduce oven temperature to 350F (175C). Bake until golden brown, about 30 minutes longer. Cover edges of turnovers with foil if they brown too quickly. Cool on wire racks. Serve at room temperature with Tipsy Yogurt Sauce. Makes 2 turnovers, 4 to 5 servings each.

Tipsy Yogurt Sauce:
In a medium bowl, combine yogurt and sour cream. Stir in brandy and lemon peel until blended. Spoon into serving dish. Sprinkle with parsley.

Variation
Substitute 1 tablespoon lemon juice combined with 2 tablespoons water for brandy in turnovers. Omit brandy in sauce. Season sauce lightly with salt and red (cayenne) pepper.

Consider how often you'll use a spice and herb blend before preparing it. Prepare only enough to last for about 3 months. Like spices and dried herbs, compounds lose fragrance and pungency after that time.

Inebriated Watermelon

Perfect ending for a picnic or cookout. Be sure to supply plain melon for the children.

1 large fully ripe watermelon
1 pint rosé wine (2 cups)

Begin preparing watermelon 2 days before serving. Set melon on its paler side, with 1 end facing you. In center of top, with a sharp knife, cut a circle or plug 2 inches in diameter, about 5 inches deep. Remove the *cylinder* of melon. Wrap in plastic wrap and refrigerate. Make 6 cuts in a sunburst pattern around plug, cutting through rind to red fruit. Place melon in a deep pan and refrigerate overnight. Pour off any juice that accumulates in cavity. Slowly pour wine into cavity. Replace plug and refrigerate melon overnight. To serve, cut into quarters, then slice. Makes 16 to 20 servings.

Variation
Substitute bourbon whiskey for the wine.

Rumtopf

Colonial housewives preserved summer fruits in this delectable way.

Granulated sugar   **Light rum, white or golden, 60 proof**
Fruit, one kind or a mixture, see below

Into a large bowl, measure equal amounts, cup for cup, of prepared fruit and sugar. Let stand 1 hour. Place in a 1- or 2-gallon glazed pottery, ceramic or glass container with a lid. Add rum to a generous 1/2 inch above fruit. Place a saucer or small plate on top of fruit, to keep it completely submerged. Cover container. If cover does not fit tightly, put a layer of plastic wrap between container and cover. Let stand undisturbed, at room temperature, at least 1 month before using. As fresh fruits come into season they can be added along with equal amounts of sugar and more rum to cover. Do not stir during standing time. Stir well before using.

Fruit for Rumtopf:
Any of the following fruits can be used on their own or in a mixture.
Strawberries: Wash and dry; cut large ones in half.
Peaches and Apricots: Dip in boiling water 1 minute, then peel. Halve apricots; slice peaches.
Melons: Halve, seed and cut into balls; or peel and cut in thin slices.
Raspberries: Sort, but do not wash.
Plums: Wash and dry. Peel, if desired; slice.
Seedless Grapes: Wash, dry and halve.
Pineapple: Peel and core; cut in chunks.
Do not use blackberries, apples, or any grapes other than seedless. Blueberries may be used, but they will give the mixture a dark, sometimes unpalatable color.

Serving Suggestions
Use Rumtopf as a sauce for ice cream or plain cake. Use the liquid to baste roast duck or goose. Serve the drained fruits as a condiment with pork, ham or game, or chop fruits and add to cake or cookies.

How to Make Inebriated Watermelon

1/In center of melon, cut out a 2-inch circle or plug, 5 inches deep.

2/Cut 6 slashes in a sunburst pattern around plug.

Peaches & Cream Tarts

A delectable custard made with Amaretto liqueur and juicy fresh peaches.

4 egg yolks, room temperature
1 tablespoon sugar
3/4 cup Amaretto liqueur
1/2 cup whipping cream, whipped
1/3 cup orange juice

3 fresh, ripe peaches
6 baked tart shells,
    about 3 inches in diameter
2/3 cup toasted slivered blanched almonds

In top of a double boiler, over simmering water, combine egg yolks and sugar. Using a whisk, stir in 1/2 cup liqueur. Cook, whisking constantly, until mixture is thick. Do not boil. Place in a medium bowl; refrigerate. When mixture is well chilled, gently fold in whipped cream. Cover and return to refrigerator. Combine orange juice and remaining 1/4 cup liqueur. Dip peaches in boiling water 1 minute, then peel, halve and pit. Place in a large bowl. Pour orange-juice mixture over peaches; refrigerate. Just before serving, drain peaches. Place a half peach in each tart shell. Spoon egg-yolk mixture over top, mounding in an attractive pattern. Sprinkle with almonds. Makes 6 servings.

Variations
When fresh fruit is not available, make these tarts with canned peaches, apricots or pitted dark sweet cherries.

Sherry-Preserved Ginger

Keeps the gingerroot fresh longer; gives the sherry a delicate flavor.

3 large pieces fresh gingerroot
Dry sherry

Cut gingerroot into a convenient size. Place in a crock or bottle. Cover with sherry. Cover and refrigerate. When a recipe calls for fresh gingerroot, cut off as much as is needed. Dry on paper towels and use as recipe directs. When a recipe calls for sherry and flavor of ginger would enhance the dish, use ginger-flavored sherry. Replace gingerroot and sherry as supply diminishes. Always store in refrigerator, up to 1 year.

Onions Trafalgar Square

Cooked British pub-style in a tart-sweet sauce, these onions accompany any meat or cheese.

1-1/2 cups Madeira wine
3/4 cup red-wine vinegar
1/2 cup packed dark-brown sugar
1/2 cup dried currants

1/8 teaspoon red (cayenne) pepper
2 lbs. small white onions, peeled
3 tablespoons vegetable oil
Salt to taste

In a large saucepan, combine Madeira, vinegar, sugar, currants and red pepper. Bring to a boil over medium-high heat, stirring constantly. Boil rapidly, uncovered, until mixture is reduced to about 1-1/4 cups. Set aside. Arrange onions in a single layer in a 12- to 14-inch skillet. Reserve extra onions to cook in second and third batches. Add oil to skillet. Cook over medium-high heat shaking pan frequently, until onions are lightly browned on all sides, about 8 minutes. Using a slotted spoon, transfer browned onions to Madeira mixture. Repeat with remaining onions. Bring onions and sauce to a boil. Reduce heat to low. Simmer, covered, until just tender, 10 to 15 minutes. Cool slightly. Season with salt to taste. Serve at room temperature. Makes 6 servings.

Poached-in-Port Apples

Serve these little rosy halfmoons of delicately spicy fruit as condiment or dessert.

4 tart apples, such as Granny Smith,
  peeled, quartered, cored
3 cups ruby port wine

1 cup sugar
1 (1-1/2-inch) cinnamon stick
English Custard, page 108, if desired

Cut each apple quarter into thirds lengthwise. In a medium saucepan, combine port, sugar and cinnamon. Bring to a boil over medium heat, stirring constantly. Reduce heat. Simmer 10 minutes. Add apple slices. Cook until barely tender, 5 to 7 minutes. Remove from heat. Let stand at room temperature, gently turning apple pieces frequently so they will absorb flavor and color of syrup evenly. Place in serving dish; refrigerate. If serving as dessert, top with English Custard. Makes 6 servings.

Variation
Bosc pears, peeled, cored and quartered lengthwise, may be substituted for apples.

Sauces & Stocks

One of the foremost rules of the world's great chefs is: *Make your own well-seasoned sauces and stocks.*

Every cook should have recipes for a few basic sauces. Homemade mayonnaise is one. You'll find the recipe, with delicious variations, in this section. Hollandaise is another. Hurry-Up Hollandaise will enhance many of your meals. Aioli, a wonderful garlic sauce, turns simple dishes into high-style delights. Tapenade is an intriguing sauce that can be used as a dip. Where would Italian meals be without Pesto? Or Greek meals without Avgolemono? Some simple sauces go with particular foods—Horseradish Cream with British boiled beef, Rémoulade Sauce with celery, Cider-Raisin Sauce with ham, and Cumberland Sauce with venison or other game.

Don't overlook sweet sauces such as English Custard, caramel, fudge or fruit.

Like any other good thing, sauces can be carried too far. One good sauce that raises a simple dish far above mediocrity makes the entire meal seem very special indeed.

There are many simple sauce-and-stock tricks of the good-cook's trade. Rice cooked in stock is far superior to that cooked in water. Dumplings poached in stock provide a happy change from rice, potatoes and noodles. Self-sauced vegetables double the flavor of the dish and rescue precious nutrients that might otherwise go down the drain.

Menu

Spring-Is-Here Dinner

Pineberry Refresher
Down-Home Pink Lemonade, page 75
Green Peppercorn Chicken, page 16
Rice Madras, page 15
Fresh Asparagus with Hurry-Up Hollandaise,
page 105
Cheese & Basil Bubbles, page 26
Strawberries with English Custard, page 109
Mount Vernon Ginger Biscuits, page 17
Coffee

Chicken Stock

Use as a soup base and in any recipe calling for white stock.

4 lbs. chicken backs, necks and wings
Cold water
8 white peppercorns
6 whole cloves
1 bay leaf

1 teaspoon dried leaf thyme
6 parsley sprigs
1 medium onion, diced
3 celery stalks, diced
1 medium carrot, diced

In a large pot, cover chicken with cold water. Bring to a boil over medium-high heat. Drain immediately. Add 4 quarts fresh cold water. Bring slowly to a boil over medium heat. Reduce heat to low. Simmer, uncovered, 30 minutes. Skim off and discard foam. Add remaining ingredients. Continue to simmer, partially covered, until liquid is reduced by half, about 3 hours. Strain. Discard bones, skin and vegetables. Cool stock, uncovered. Pour into quart or pint containers with tight-fitting lids. Cover and store in refrigerator up to 2 days, or in freezer up to 4 months. Makes about 2 quarts.

Beef Stock

Base for many soups and sauces; use whenever recipe calls for brown stock.

4 lbs. beef bones and meat trimmings
1 Bouquet Garni, page 133
4 qts. cold water
1 cup dry red wine, if desired

3 celery stalks, chopped
1 large onion, chopped
1 large carrot, chopped
1/2 teaspoon garlic juice

Preheat oven to 450F (230C). On a large baking sheet with raised sides, spread bones and trimmings in a single layer. Bake until deeply browned, about 1 hour. Prepare Bouquet Garni. Transfer bones, trimmings and accumulated juice to a large pot. Add cold water. Bring just to boiling point. Skim off and discard foam. Add remaining ingredients. Reduce heat to low. Simmer, partially covered, until liquid is reduced by half, about 3 hours. Strain. Discard bones and vegetables. Cool stock, uncovered. Pour into pint or quart containers with tight-fitting lids. Cover and store in refrigerator up to 4 days or in freezer up to 5 months. Makes about 2 quarts.

Variation

Veal Stock: Substitute veal bones for beef bones. Omit step of browning bones. Substitute white wine for red wine. Stock will be pale in color. Store in refrigerator up to 2 days or in freezer up to 2 months.

Regular canned broth (14-1/2-ounce can) can be substituted for homemade stock, measure for measure. If using a 10-ounce can of condensed broth, dilute it with 3/4 cup water before measuring; undiluted, it will be too salty.

Greek Vegetable Soup

Turn a simple soup into a one-dish wonder with the help of zesty Skordalia.

Skordalia, page 102
6 cups Chicken Stock, opposite page,
   or canned chicken broth
1/2 lb. mushrooms, thinly sliced
1-1/2 cups fresh spinach,
   washed, stems removed

2 tomatoes, peeled, seeded, coarsely chopped
6 hard-cooked eggs, shelled,
   coarsely chopped
Salt and ground black pepper to taste

Prepare Skordalia; let stand at room temperature. In a large saucepan, bring stock or broth to a boil over medium-high heat. Add mushrooms. Reduce heat to low. Simmer, covered, 5 minutes. Tear spinach leaves into bite-size pieces. Add torn spinach leaves and tomatoes to broth mixture. Cover and simmer 1 minute. Add hard-cooked eggs. Season to taste with salt and pepper. Remove from heat. For main-dish servings, spoon 2 tablespoons Skordalia into each of 6 soup bowls; for smaller servings spoon 1 tablespoon Skordalia into each bowl. Ladle soup over Skordalia. Serve immediately. Makes 6 main-dish servings or 12 starter servings.

White Sauce

Use this medium-thick version to sauce vegetables or to make creamed dishes.

2 tablespoons butter or margarine
2 tablespoons all-purpose flour

1 cup milk
1/2 teaspoon salt

In a heavy saucepan, melt butter or margarine over low heat; do not brown. Remove from heat. Rapidly whisk in flour. Return to heat. Gradually add milk, whisking constantly. Heat, stirring with whisk, until mixture bubbles and thickens. Continue to cook 2 minutes, whisking constantly. Stir in salt. Recipe may be doubled or tripled. Makes 1 cup.

Variations
Seasoned Sauce: In addition to salt, add 1/8 teaspoon ground white pepper, 1/2 teaspoon onion powder and 1/4 teaspoon celery salt.

Thin White Sauce or Base for Cream Soups: Reduce butter to 1 tablespoon. Reduce flour to 1 tablespoon.

Thick White Sauce or Base for Croquettes & Soufflés: Increase butter to 3 tablespoons. Increase flour to 3 tablespoons.

French Cream Sauce: Reduce milk to 1/2 cup. Add 1/2 cup half and half or whipping cream.

Sauce Velouté: Reduce milk to 1/2 cup. Add 1/2 cup Chicken Stock, opposite page, or canned chicken broth.

Cheese Sauce: At end of cooking time, stir in 1 cup shredded Cheddar or Swiss cheese (4 ounces) until melted. Do not boil after adding cheese.

Dippers & Snacks with Tapenade

A flavorful appetizer feast to please the most devoted snackers.

Tapenade, see below
2 (10-oz.) pkgs. frozen artichoke hearts,
   cooked, drained
2 cups small whole red radishes
1 small head cauliflower
1 (10-oz.) pkg. frozen snow peas, thawed
2 medium cucumbers
2 medium zucchini
1 (1-pint) basket cherry tomatoes

12 green onions, trimmed
3 large carrots, peeled
1/2 lb. provolone cheese, trimmed,
   cut in small fingers
1/2 lb. Tilsit or Appenzeller cheese,
   cut in small fingers
1 (7- to 9-oz.) pkg. grissini
   (very thin bread sticks)

Make all preparations in advance. Prepare and refrigerate Tapenade. Refrigerate artichoke hearts. Trim radishes. Break cauliflower into flowerets. Immerse snow peas in very hot water 1 minute; drain well. Do not peel cucumbers unless waxed. Cut cucumbers in half lengthwise, then crosswise. Remove seeds with tip of a teaspoon. Cut cucumber quarters into fingers. Cut off stem and blossom ends of zucchini. Cut in half lengthwise and crosswise, then cut into fingers. Wash and drain cherry tomatoes. Refrigerate all vegetables in separate containers. Using a swivel-blade vegetable parer, cut long, thin strips of carrot. Place in a bowl of ice water. Refrigerate. After preparing cheeses, wrap each separately in foil, making airtight packages. Store in refrigerator. Carefully break each breadstick into 3 pieces; set aside at room temperature. To serve, place bowl of Tapenade in center or at 1 end of a large platter. Arrange vegetables, cheeses and grissini pieces on the platter in an attractive pattern. Makes 12 to 16 servings.

Tapenade

From France, a richly rewarding sauce for raw vegetables, cheeses, eggs and crackers.

1 (12-oz.) can light tuna, drained
1 (8-oz.) can pitted ripe olives,
   drained, quartered
1 (2-oz.) can anchovies, drained
1/2 cup drained capers
6 hard-cooked eggs, shelled, quartered

2 garlic cloves, minced
1/4 cup lemon juice
1/2 cup olive oil
Coarsely ground black pepper
Parsley sprigs

In blender or food processor, combine tuna, olives, anchovies and capers. With several on-and-off bursts of medium speed, process until coarsely chopped. Add eggs and garlic. Again, process just until coarsely chopped. Add lemon juice and olive oil. Process just until mixture is blended. Season to taste with pepper. Spoon into a serving bowl. Tuck small sprigs of parsley around edge. Refrigerate until serving time. Makes about 4 cups.

Cumberland Sauce

This is the classic sauce to serve with ham and game, particularly venison.

1 teaspoon dry mustard	2 teaspoons cornstarch
1 tablespoon brown sugar	2 tablespoons cold water
1/4 teaspoon ground ginger	1/4 cup tart red-currant jelly
1/4 teaspoon salt	1 tablespoon grated orange peel
1/4 teaspoon ground cloves	1/4 cup orange juice
1-1/2 cups ruby port wine	2 tablespoons lemon juice

In a medium saucepan, combine mustard, sugar, ginger, salt, cloves and port. Bring to a boil over medium-high heat. Reduce heat to low. Simmer, covered, 8 minutes. Stir cornstarch into cold water until smooth. Stir into simmering sauce. Simmer 2 minutes. Stir in jelly, orange peel, orange juice and lemon juice. Continue to simmer, stirring constantly, until jelly is melted and sauce is blended. Serve hot. Makes about 2 cups.

Variations

Add 1/2 cup raisins or blanched slivered almonds, or both, to simmering port mixture before adding cornstarch mixture.

For an elegant finishing touch, stir in 2 tablespoons Grand Marnier just before serving.

Skordalia

Try on hot or cold vegetables and in any soup or braised meat dish.

1 tablespoon chopped garlic	1/4 cup fine dry breadcrumbs
1/4 teaspoon salt	1/2 cup crumbled feta cheese (2 oz.)
1 cup fresh parsley	1 tablespoon dried leaf oregano
1 cup vegetable oil	1 tablespoon drained capers
1/4 cup lemon juice	

In blender, process garlic, salt, parsley, 1/2 cup oil and lemon juice at medium speed, 45 seconds. Stop and scrape down side of container as necessary. Add remaining 1/2 cup oil, breadcrumbs, cheese, oregano and capers. Process 1 minute longer, scraping down side of container as necessary. Serve immediately or cover and refrigerate. Makes about 1-2/3 cups.

Rémoulade Sauce

Use this versatile sauce to dress fish, cold meat or poultry and vegetables.

1 cup Blender Mayonnaise, opposite page, or commercial mayonnaise	2 teaspoons Dijon-style mustard
	1 teaspoon finely snipped fresh parsley
1 tablespoon finely chopped cucumber pickle	1/2 teaspoon dried leaf chervil
	1/4 teaspoon dried leaf tarragon
1 tablespoon chopped drained capers	1/2 teaspoon anchovy paste

In a small bowl, combine all ingredients. Mix well. Serve immediately, or cover and refrigerate. Makes about 1-1/3 cups.

Blender Mayonnaise

Trouble-free, delicate and lemony—particularly good on chicken and seafood salads.

1 egg
1 cup vegetable oil
2 tablespoons lemon juice

1 drop hot-pepper sauce
1/2 teaspoon Dijon-style mustard
1/4 teaspoon salt

In blender, process egg, 1/4 cup oil, lemon juice, pepper sauce, mustard and salt at high speed until blended, about 30 seconds. Remove top of blender. Continuing to process at high speed, slowly add remaining 3/4 cup oil. Continue to process until thick and smooth. Serve immediately or pour into a 1-cup container with a tight-fitting lid. Refrigerate up to 1 week. Makes about 1 cup.

Variations

Double-Lemon Mayonnaise: Add 1/2 teaspoon grated lemon peel before first processing.

Chive Mayonnaise: Add 1 tablespoon finely snipped fresh chives before first processing.

Tarragon Mayonnaise: Add 2 tablespoons finely snipped fresh tarragon or 2-1/4 teaspoons crumbled dried leaf tarragon before first processing.

Caper Mayonnaise: Add 1-1/2 tablespoons well-drained capers before first processing.

Robust Italian-Style Mayonnaise: Substitute olive oil for vegetable oil and red-wine vinegar for lemon juice. Increase hot-pepper sauce to 3 drops and mustard to 1 teaspoon.

Pesto

Use this pungent green sauce in soups and dips, with pasta or to season broiled meats.

3/4 cup pine nuts
2 cups packed fresh basil
1/2 teaspoon salt
1/8 teaspoon ground black pepper

1/2 cup grated Parmesan cheese (1-1/2 oz.)
1/2 cup grated Romano cheese (1-1/2 oz.)
2 large garlic cloves, peeled, quartered
1/2 cup olive oil

In blender or food processor, process pine nuts, basil, salt, pepper, cheeses and garlic at high speed, just until smooth. Gradually pour in oil, continuing to process just until smooth. Serve immediately or cover and refrigerate up to 5 days or freeze up to 5 months. Makes about 1-1/3 cups.

Variations

Mock Pesto I: Substitute 2 cups chopped fresh spinach leaves and 2 teaspoons crumbled dried leaf basil for fresh basil.

Mock Pesto II: Substitute 1-3/4 cups finely snipped fresh parsley and 2 tablespoons crumbled dried leaf basil for fresh basil.

To Use Pesto:

Combine 2 tablespoons Pesto, 1/2 cup mayonnaise and 1 cup dairy sour cream or plain yogurt. Serve as a dip with fingers of cheese and assorted raw vegetables.

In a screwtop jar, shake together 6 tablespoons Pesto, 1/3 cup red-wine vinegar and 2/3 cup olive oil. Use to dress tomatoes or green salad, or as a marinade for small mushrooms.

Add 1/3 cup Pesto to 2 cups spaghetti sauce. Serve over pasta, or as a sauce for omelets.

Combine 1/4 cup Pesto, 1/2 cup melted butter or margarine and 1 teaspoon lemon juice. Use as a dip for hot cooked artichokes, or as a sauce for cooked shrimp or lobster.

How to Make Braised Leeks Hollandaise

1/Pierce center of foil with a sharp fork. Press foil into a skillet.

2/Drain leeks by holding edges of foil and lifting foil and leeks from skillet.

Cider-Raisin Sauce

Serve this sauce with hot or cold ham, cold sliced tongue or cooked liver.

1-1/2 cups apple cider
1/2 cup raisins, halved
1/4 cup packed brown sugar
2 tablespoons cornstarch
1/8 teaspoon salt

8 whole cloves
1 (2-inch) cinnamon stick
1/4 lemon, unpeeled, diced
1 tablespoon butter or margarine

In a small bowl, pour cider over raisins. Let stand at room temperature 1 hour. In a medium saucepan, combine sugar, cornstarch and salt. Stir in cider mixture. In a 5-inch square of double-thickness cheesecloth, combine cloves, cinnamon and lemon. Tie with kitchen string; suspend in sauce mixture. Stirring gently, cook sauce over medium heat 10 minutes. Remove bag of spices. Stir in butter or margarine until melted. Serve sauce very hot. Makes about 2 cups.

Braised Leeks Hollandaise

Try cooking asparagus or green onions by this ingenious method.

8 medium leeks
Salt and ground white pepper

Hurry-Up Hollandaise Sauce, see below

Remove roots and all dark-green portions from tops of leeks. Wash leeks under running water to remove any sand or dirt. Tear off a 24-inch-long sheet of foil. Near center of foil, pierce 5 or 6 times with a sharp fork. Press foil into a 12-inch skillet, shaping so end pieces extend over side of skillet. Arrange leeks on foil. Add water to cover. Bring to a boil over medium-high heat. Reduce heat to low. Cover. Simmer until leeks are tender, 10 to 20 minutes depending on size. Drain by lifting and bringing together ends of foil, letting liquid drip through holes into skillet. Arrange drained leeks on a warm platter. Sprinkle lightly with salt and white pepper; keep warm. Prepare Hurry-Up Hollandaise. If more liquid has drained from leeks, remove by blotting with paper towels. Spoon sauce over leeks. Serve immediately. Makes 4 servings.

Hurry-Up Hollandaise Sauce

A golden, easy-to-make sauce to use with any dish that a sauce will improve.

1/2 cup butter or margarine
3 egg yolks
1-1/2 tablespoons lemon juice

1/4 teaspoon salt
1/8 teaspoon red (cayenne) pepper

Heat butter or margarine in a small saucepan over low heat. In blender, combine egg yolks, lemon juice, salt and red pepper. Cover. With several on-and-off bursts of medium speed, process just until blended. When butter or margarine begins to bubble but has not begun to brown, remove center of blender cover. Slowly add melted butter or margarine while blending on medium speed. Turn off blender as soon as all is added. Serve immediately. Makes 3/4 cup.

Horseradish Cream

In England, boiled beef is considered naked when served without horseradish.

1/2 cup whipping cream
3 tablespoons lemon juice or
  white-wine vinegar
1/4 teaspoon salt
1/8 teaspoon sweet paprika

2 tablespoons grated fresh horseradish or
  well-drained prepared horseradish
1/4 teaspoon onion juice
3 tablespoons mayonnaise, if desired

In a small bowl, beat cream with electric mixer until thick. Gradually beat in lemon juice or vinegar, salt and paprika. By hand, stir in horseradish, onion juice and mayonnaise, if desired, until blended. Serve at room temperature. Makes about 1-1/4 cups.

Aioli

Delicious seasoning for shellfish, vegetables and soups.

15 large garlic cloves, minced
1 hard-cooked egg yolk
2 eggs
4 teaspoons lemon juice

2 tablespoons vegetable oil
2 cups olive oil
Salt to taste

In a small bowl, combine garlic, egg yolk, eggs and 2 teaspoons lemon juice. Beat with a fork to blend. With electric mixer at high speed, beat in vegetable oil a few drops at a time. Beat until mixture thickens slightly and turns a creamy yellow. Beat in remaining 2 teaspoons lemon juice. Gradually add olive oil, pouring in a very thin stream while beating constantly. Season to taste with salt. Serve immediately or cover and refrigerate. Remove from refrigerator about 1 hour before serving. Serve Aioli at room temperature. Makes about 3 cups.

Serving Suggestions
Serve as a sauce for any fish or cooked vegetable, as an appetizer dip with raw vegetables or as a garnish for strong-flavored soups such as cabbage or onion. Aioli can also be used as a spread for bread—preferably rye or pumpernickel—served as is or as a base for ham or beef sandwiches.

Avgolemono Sauce

Perfect accompaniment to cabbage, broccoli, cauliflower and Brussels sprouts.

3 eggs
2 drops hot-pepper sauce
1 cup cold Chicken Stock, page 98,
  or canned chicken broth

3 tablespoons lemon juice
Salt, if desired

In a heavy saucepan, beat eggs with a whisk just until whites and yolks are combined. Whisk in pepper sauce, stock or broth and lemon juice. Cook over low heat, whisking constantly, until sauce thickens enough to coat a spoon; do not boil. Taste and add salt if desired. Use immediately. Makes about 1-1/2 cups.

Tartare Sauce

Serve with any plain fish dish—baked, broiled or fried.

1 cup Blender Mayonnaise,
  page 103, or commercial mayonnaise
1 teaspoon Dijon-style mustard
1 tablespoon finely snipped fresh parsley
1 tablespoon minced shallots,
  or 1 tablespoon minced green onions
  and 1 drop garlic juice

2 drops hot-pepper sauce
1 tablespoon chopped sweet pickle
1 tablespoon chopped green olives
1 hard-cooked egg, finely chopped
1 tablespoon chopped drained capers
1 tablespoon lemon juice
Salt to taste

In a small bowl, combine all ingredients. Refrigerate. Makes about 1-1/3 cups.

Oriental Sauces

These dips and toppings will give excellent flavor to your home-cooked dishes.

Hot Mustard Sauce

1/4 cup boiling water
1/4 cup dry mustard

In a small bowl, stir water into mustard to make a smooth paste. Let stand at room temperature 1 hour to develop a very hot mustard flavor. Serve at room temperature. Makes about 1/3 cup.

Serving suggestion
Use sparingly as a dip for spring rolls and Chinese barbecued meats.

Mustard Sauce

2 tablespoons hot water
3 tablespoons dry mustard
1 tablespoon toasted sesame seeds

3/4 cup soy sauce
1/4 teaspoon garlic juice
6 tablespoons whipped cream

In a small bowl, stir water into mustard to make a smooth paste. In blender, combine mustard mixture, sesame seeds, soy sauce and garlic juice. Process at high speed 1 minute. Transfer mixture to a small bowl. By hand, gently stir in whipped cream. Serve at room temperature. Makes about 1 cup.

Serving suggestion
Serve with dim sum, Oriental beef dishes or stir-fried Chinese cabbage.

Plum Sauce

1 tablespoon vegetable oil
1 medium onion, cut in eighths
2 tablespoons cornstarch
3/4 cup sugar
3/4 cup white vinegar

2 lbs. ripe red-fleshed plums,
    quartered, pitted
1/2 teaspoon salt
1/8 teaspoon almond extract

In a medium saucepan, heat oil over medium heat. Add onion. Cook until soft but not browned; set aside. In a small bowl, combine cornstarch and sugar. Stir in vinegar. Stir into onions in saucepan. Cook and stir constantly over medium heat until thickened. Add plums, salt and almond extract. Cook over low heat, stirring frequently, until plums are tender, 15 to 25 minutes. Process half of the mixture at a time in blender, until smooth. Serve hot or at room temperature. Makes about 2-1/2 cups.

Serving suggestion
Traditional dip for appetizers such as spareribs and bite-size chicken pieces.

Easy Plum Sauce

1-1/2 cups plum preserves or plum jam
2 teaspoons onion juice
1/2 teaspoon salt

2 tablespoons white vinegar
1/4 teaspoon ground ginger

In a medium saucepan, combine all ingredients. Stirring constantly, cook over low heat until mixture is blended. Serve hot or at room temperature. Makes 1-1/2 cups.

Serving suggestion
Use as dip with savory meat appetizers.

Ginza Ginger Sauce

1 small onion, sliced
1/2 cup soy sauce
1/4 cup white-wine vinegar

1-inch piece fresh gingerroot,
    or 1/4 teaspoon ground ginger
1/2 teaspoon sugar

In blender, process all ingredients at medium speed until onion and ginger are minced. Serve at room temperature. Makes about 3/4 cup.

Serving Suggestions
Serve with stir-fried chicken or fish dishes, or as a dip for appetizers.

How to Make Tipsy Cake with English Custard

1/Cook custard until thick enough to coat a spoon.

2/Spread marmalade mixture over cake; top with custard. Garnish with orange sections.

English Custard

The British way to top fresh or canned fruit and hearty puddings.

1-1/2 cups milk, scalded
5 tablespoons sugar
1/8 teaspoon salt

4 egg yolks, slightly beaten
1 teaspoon vanilla extract

In top of a double boiler, combine milk, sugar and salt. Place directly over heat. Stir until sugar dissolves. Gradually stir 1/2 cup hot mixture into egg yolks. Stir egg-yolk mixture into remaining hot mixture. Place over simmering water. Stirring constantly, cook until thickened, about 3 minutes. Stir in vanilla. Cool slightly; then refrigerate, if desired. Serve hot or cold. Makes 2 cups.

Variations

For a thinner custard, increase milk to 2 cups.

Substitute lemon, orange, coffee, coconut, nutmeg or maple extract for vanilla extract. Start with 1/2 teaspoon extract; taste before adding more.

Tipsy Cake with English Custard

Delectable way to serve leftover pound or sponge cake.

English Custard, opposite page
4 (1/4-inch) slices pound cake
1/2 cup tart orange marmalade

1 tablespoon brandy or dry sherry
1 (11-oz.) can mandarin-orange sections,
  drained

Prepare English Custard. To serve, place 1 slice cake on each of 4 individual serving dishes. In a small bowl, mix marmalade with brandy or sherry. Spread lightly over each piece of cake. Spoon custard over marmalade mixture. Decorate with orange sections. Serve immediately. Makes 4 servings.

Variation
Substitute raspberry, strawberry or cherry preserves for orange marmalade.

Poached Pears Caramel

Delicate pears bathed in a gloriously rich sauce.

1-1/4 cups Caramel-Butter Sauce,
  see below
4 large Bosc or comice pears
1 teaspoon white vinegar

1/2 cup sugar
1 cup cold water
Boiling water, if needed
Fresh mint sprigs, if desired

Prepare Caramel-Butter Sauce; keep warm. Peel, halve and core pears. In a large saucepan, combine vinegar, sugar and cold water. Bring to a boil over medium-high heat, stirring frequently, until sugar dissolves. Reduce heat to low. Add pears, cut-side down. Add boiling water if liquid does not cover pears. Simmer over low heat until pears are tender when pierced with tip of a sharp knife, about 10 minutes. Do not overcook. With a slotted spoon, transfer pears to individual serving dishes. Spoon Caramel-Butter Sauce over pears. Garnish with mint, if desired. Makes 4 servings.

Caramel-Butter Sauce

Rich sauce to use—but sparingly—on cake, fruit or ice cream.

1-1/2 cups whipping cream
1 cup butter or margarine

3/4 cup sugar

In a medium saucepan, warm cream over low heat. In a heavy medium saucepan, combine butter or margarine and sugar. Place over medium heat. Stirring frequently, cook until mixture is golden brown. Watch carefully to prevent mixture from burning. Using a wire whisk, gradually stir in warm cream. Simmer over low heat, stirring, until mixture is smooth, 3 to 4 minutes. Store extra sauce, covered, in refrigerator up to 1 week; reheat to serve. Makes about 2-1/2 cups.

Compound Butters

Until relatively modern times, butter-making was strictly a home project. The family cow, camel or goat supplied milk which was served to children, churned into butter or made into cheese. Fresh-churned butter was wrapped in linen or in fresh green leaves and sold in the village square on market days.

The fact that butter was exceedingly perishable was its greatest drawback. Farmers learned that adding salt to their butter prolonged its life, and herdsmen discovered that turning their butter into *ghee (clarified butter)* accomplished the same purpose. Butter-making turned from a home project into a cottage industry and then into a nationwide business.

There are many things to be done with butter besides spreading it on bread or toast and using it in baking and cooking. Butter takes on a special magic when flavored in sweet or savory ways to make compound butters. Orange-Honey Butter,

for example, doubles the pleasure of homemade waffles, pancakes, muffins and other hot breads. The same is true of Strawberry-Brandy Butter, Toffee Butter, Sweet Lime Butter and many others.

Savory butters have their place in the menu. Cheddar Butter, Mustard Butter and herb-flavored and savory butters make wonderful spreads for sandwiches and add zest to vegetables. Savory butters top steaks, dress seafood and glorify chicken.

Whipped butter is a pleasure to use. It goes further and spreads more readily than the solid kind.

All of the sweet or savory compound butters that follow are quick and easy to make. They will keep four days at cool room temperature or longer in the refrigerator. Most can be frozen for up to two months. All are excellent to have on hand to dress up simple foods. Margarine may be substituted for butter.

Menu

Membership Drive Afternoon Tea

Home-Whipped Butter

Use as superior spread for toast or hot or cold breads, or as a base for flavored butters.

1 lb. butter or margarine,
  unsalted or salted, room temperature

1 egg
1/4 cup cold whipping cream

In large bowl of electric mixer, combine butter or margarine and egg. Beat at low speed with electric mixer until blended. Increase speed to high; beat 5 minutes. Reduce speed to low. Gradually beat in cream until blended. At high speed, beat until very light and fluffy, 10 to 15 minutes. Spoon into two 1-pound containers with tight-fitting lids. Store in refrigerator up to 4 days or in freezer up to 2 months. Makes about 4 cups.

Chervil Butter   Photo on cover and page 25.

For all fish—self-caught, from the market or out of a can.

1/2 cup butter or margarine,
  room temperature
1/4 teaspoon grated lemon peel

2 teaspoons ground chervil
2 drops hot-pepper sauce

In a small bowl, cream butter or margarine and lemon peel until fluffy. Add chervil and pepper sauce. Beat until light and blended. Serve immediately or cover and refrigerate. Remove from refrigerator about 20 minutes before serving. Makes about 1/2 cup.

Herb-Buttered Roasting Ears

Grill fresh corn with savory butter and a bonus of zesty cheese.

1/2 cup butter or margarine,
  room temperature
1 garlic clove, minced
1-1/2 teaspoons snipped fresh basil,
  or 3/4 teaspoon dried leaf basil,
  crumbled

1/2 teaspoon dried leaf oregano, crumbled
1/4 teaspoon salt
1/8 teaspoon ground black pepper
4 large ears of corn, husked
1/2 cup grated Romano cheese (1-1/2 oz.)

In a small bowl, combine butter or margarine, garlic, basil, oregano, salt and pepper. Beat until blended. Divide mixture evenly among corn ears, spreading on all sides. Wrap each ear in foil, making a lengthwise drugstore fold and turning up ends securely. Ears must be tightly enclosed so butter will not leak out. Roast on a grill about 4 inches from coals until tender, 15 to 20 minutes, turning every 5 minutes. Open foil. Sprinkle corn with cheese. Serve immediately. Makes 4 servings.

Variation
Instead of on a grill, corn may be roasted in a preheated 350F (175C) oven 20 to 25 minutes.

Choice-of-Butters Burgers

Use the butters to season other meats or poultry, and to dress vegetables.

Cheddar Butter, opposite page
Mustard Butter, see below
2 lbs. lean ground beef
1 teaspoon salt

1/2 cup ice water
6 slices firm white bread,
    toasted, crusts trimmed

In advance, prepare and refrigerate or freeze Cheddar Butter and Mustard Butter. In a medium bowl, lightly combine beef, salt and ice water. Shape into 6 patties. Cook in skillet or on a grill to desired doneness. Place toast slices on 6 individual plates. Place a beef patty on each slice of toast. Top each with a 1/4-inch slice of Cheddar Butter or Mustard Butter. Makes 6 servings.

Mustard Butter

Great to have on hand for dressing beef or pork or cabbage-family vegetables.

1/2 cup butter or margarine,
    room temperature
2 teaspoons lemon juice
2 tablespoons Dijon-style mustard

2 teaspoons finely snipped
    fresh parsley
1/8 teaspoon finely ground black pepper

In a medium bowl, combine all ingredients. Beat until fluffy. On heavy-duty foil, shape mixture into a log about 1 inch in diameter. Refrigerate or freeze until ready to serve. To serve, cut into 1/4-inch slices. Refrigerate unused mixture up to 4 days or freeze up to 2 weeks. Makes one 8- to 10-inch log.

Basil Butter

Basil and tomatoes make perfect partners, so serve them together.

1/2 cup butter or margarine,
    room temperature
1/4 teaspoon garlic juice

1 teaspoon dried leaf basil, crumbled
2 drops hot-pepper sauce

In a small bowl, cream butter or margarine until fluffy. Stir in garlic juice, basil and pepper sauce until blended. Serve immediately or cover and refrigerate. Makes about 1/2 cup.

How to Make Cheddar Butter

1/Beat butter mixture until light and fluffy. Fold in shredded cheese. Shape into a log; refrigerate or freeze.

2/Cut cold butter log into slices. Serve with vegetable, meat dishes or in pasta casseroles.

Cheddar Butter

Cheese-and-herb combination for any beef dish or many vegetables.

1/2 cup butter or margarine,
   room temperature
1/4 teaspoon dried leaf basil
1/4 teaspoon dried leaf thyme
1/4 teaspoon onion powder

1/4 teaspoon dried leaf oregano
1/8 teaspoon garlic powder
1 cup shredded Cheddar cheese (4 oz.)
1 teaspoon lemon juice

In a medium bowl, combine butter or margarine, basil, thyme, onion powder, oregano and garlic powder. Beat until fluffy. Blend in cheese and lemon juice. On heavy-duty foil, shape mixture into a log about 1 inch in diameter. Refrigerate or freeze until ready to serve. To serve, cut into 1/4-inch slices. Refrigerate unused mixture up to 4 days or freeze up to to 2 weeks. Make one 8- to 10-inch log.

Savory Butter Variations

To 3/4 cup Home-Whipped Butter, page 111, add any of the following:

2 tablespoons caraway seeds

1/4 cup finely snipped chives

1/4 cup finely snipped fresh parsley or
fresh basil and 1/2 teaspoon lemon juice

3 tablespoons finely snipped fresh tarragon
and 1/4 teaspoon lemon juice

2 teaspoons curry powder and
1/4 cup flaked unsweetened coconut

1 tablespoon onion juice and
2 tablespoons grated Parmesan cheese

1 teaspoon garlic juice,
1/4 teaspoon lemon juice and
1/4 teaspoon celery seeds

3 tablespoons drained prepared horseradish

3 tablespoons chopped chutney

1 tablespoon anchovy paste and
1/4 teaspoon lemon juice

2 tablespoons chili sauce and
3 drops hot-pepper sauce

2 tablespoons ketchup,
1/4 teaspoon lemon juice and
1/8 teaspoon red (cayenne) pepper

2 tablespoons well-drained India relish and
1/2 teaspoon onion powder

2 hard-cooked eggs, finely chopped,
1/4 teaspoon salt and
1/8 teaspoon red (cayenne) pepper

1/2 cup shredded Cheddar cheese (2 oz.) and
1/8 teaspoon dry mustard

2 tablespoons mashed feta cheese,
1/4 teaspoon garlic juice and
2 tablespoons finely chopped ripe olives

In each case, beat combined ingredients until blended. Serve immediately or cover and refrigerate. Use to dress meat, fish, poultry, vegetables or to spread on bread for hearty sandwiches.

Pasta Butter

For all types of pasta, and to season mashed or baked potatoes.

1/2 cup butter or margarine,
room temperature
1/2 teaspoon dried leaf oregano, crumbled

1/4 teaspoon garlic juice
1/4 teaspoon dried leaf marjoram, crumbled

In a small bowl, cream butter or margarine until fluffy. Add oregano, garlic juice and marjoram; stir until blended. Serve immediately or cover and refrigerate. Makes about 1/2 cup.

Savory Steak Butter

Try this on roast beef, pot roast or even hamburgers.

1 cup butter or margarine, room temperature
1/4 cup Worcestershire sauce
3/4 teaspoon anchovy paste
1/2 cup finely snipped fresh parsley

1/8 teaspoon sweet paprika
1/8 teaspoon garlic powder
1/8 teaspoon finely ground black pepper

In blender or food processor, combine butter or margarine, Worcestershire sauce and anchovy paste. Process at medium speed until blended. Add parsley, paprika, garlic powder and pepper. Process until blended. On heavy-duty foil, shape mixture into a log about 1 inch in diameter. Freeze until ready to serve. To serve, cut into 1/4- to 1/2-inch slices. Refrigerate unused mixture up to 4 days or freeze up to 2 months. Makes one 14-inch log.

Elegant Eggplant

Butter-broiling creates a vegetable dish everyone will enjoy.

1 large or 2 medium eggplants
Salt

Basil Butter, page 112

Peel eggplant or not, as you prefer. Cut in 8 slices. On a flat surface, place a piece of waxed paper large enough to accommodate eggplant in a single layer. Sprinkle paper liberally with salt. Place eggplant on salt. Sprinkle salt generously over tops of eggplant slices. Let stand at room temperature 1 hour. Prepare Basil Butter; let stand at room temperature. Preheat broiler if manufacturer directs. Generously butter a large baking sheet. Rinse eggplant slices well under cold running water. Dry gently with paper towels. Butter both sides of each slice with Basil Butter, as if buttering bread. Place on baking sheet in a single layer. Broil about 4 inches from source of heat until lightly browned, 3 to 4 minutes. With a wide spatula, turn eggplant. Broil second side until lightly browned and tender. Makes 4 servings.

Chili-Garlic Butter

Makes the ultimate garlic bread; also good on corn bread and to season vegetables.

1/2 cup butter or margarine,
  room temperature

1 large garlic clove, minced
1-1/2 teaspoons chili powder

In a small bowl, cream butter or margarine until fluffy. Add garlic and chili powder; stir to blend. Use immediately or cover and refrigerate. Makes about 1/2 cup.

New Potatoes Danish-Style

Enchance the flavor of tender, moist potatoes.

Danish Dill Butter, see below   **1 teaspoon salt**
12 small, uniform red-skinned potatoes

Prepare and refrigerate Danish Dill Butter. Wash potatoes. Pare a strip around center of each, but otherwise do not peel. Place in a medium saucepan. Add water to cover. Add salt. Cook over medium heat until tender when pierced with the tip of a sharp knife, 15 to 20 minutes. Drain well. Place in a warm serving dish. Top with dollops of Danish Dill Butter. Serve immediately. Makes 6 servings.

Danish Dill Butter   Photo on page 41.

For any fish or vegetable, but it's best on grilled salmon or broiled tomatoes.

2 hard-cooked eggs, shelled   **1/2 teaspoon salt**
1/2 cup butter or margarine,   **1/4 teaspoon sweet paprika**
**   room temperature**   **1/8 teaspoon ground white pepper**
4 teaspoons dried dillweed

Halve hard-cooked eggs. Place yolks in a small sieve and whites in a small dish. With a fork, mash whites until they are finely chopped; set aside. Into a small bowl, press yolks through sieve, using back of a spoon. Add butter or margarine to sieved egg yolks; beat until fluffy. Add dillweed, salt, paprika and pepper. Beat until fluffy and blended. Gently stir in chopped egg whites. Serve immediately or cover and refrigerate. Makes about 3/4 cup.

Brown Butter

This is the French beurre noisette, a perfect finishing touch for fish or vegetables.

1/4 cup butter or margarine   **1 teaspoon white-wine vinegar**
1/2 teaspoon onion juice or onion powder

In a small saucepan, melt butter or margarine over medium-low heat. Continue to cook, swirling pan, until foam develops, then subsides. Butter or margarine will be golden brown. Stir in onion juice or powder and vinegar. Serve immediately. Makes about 1/4 cup.

How to Make New Potatoes Danish-Style

1/Cut a strip of peel from around center of each potato. Cook potatoes in water to cover.

2/To make Danish Dill Butter, press egg yolks through a fine strainer into a small bowl.

Cauliflower Mimosa

Pretty as a spring bouquet—and every bit as delicious.

1 medium head cauliflower
Brown Butter, opposite page
2 hard-cooked eggs, shelled, halved

1/4 cup finely snipped fresh parsley
1/4 cup fine dry breadcrumbs

Remove leaves from cauliflower. Trim stem even with bottom of head. Cook whole head in a large pan of boiling salted water until crisp-tender, 10 to 20 minutes. Drain on paper towels. While cauliflower cooks, prepare Brown Butter; keep warm over lowest heat. Place egg yolks in a small sieve; set aside. Chop egg whites coarsely. Combine with parsley and breadcrumbs. Place drained cauliflower in a warm serving dish just large enough to accommodate it. Pour Brown Butter over cauliflower. Sprinkle evenly with breadcrumb mixture. With back of a spoon, press egg yolks through sieve over cauliflower. Serve immediately. Makes 4 to 6 servings.

Maple Butter

A favorite flavor from New England that will delight weekend brunchers.

1/2 cup butter, room temperature
3 tablespoons sifted powdered sugar

1 teaspoon maple extract

In a small bowl, beat butter with electric mixer at medium speed, until fluffy. Beat in powdered sugar and maple extract. Turn speed to high; beat 1 minute. Serve immediately or cover and refrigerate. If refrigerated, let stand at room temperature about 20 minutes before serving. Makes about 2/3 cup.

Sweet Butter Variations

To 3/4 cup unsalted Home-Whipped Butter, page 111, add any of the following:

1/4 cup finely chopped fresh mint and
  1/2 teaspoon lemon juice

1 tablespoon lemon juice and
  2 teaspoons grated lemon peel

1 tablespoon orange juice and
  1 tablespoon poppy seeds

1 tablespoon orange juice,
  4 teaspoons grated orange peel and
  1/4 teaspoon ground nutmeg

2 tablespoons powdered sugar and
  1/2 teaspoon ground cinnamon or
  1/4 teaspoon ground mace or
  1 teaspoon vanilla extract

2 tablespoons honey and
  1/4 teaspoon ground mace

7 or 8 ripe strawberries, mashed,
  and 1 tablespoon powdered sugar

20 ripe raspberries, mashed,
  1 tablespoon powdered sugar and
  1/8 teaspoon lemon juice

3 tablespoons finely chopped walnuts,
  pecans, filberts or pistachios

3 tablespoons toasted sesame seeds

2 tablespoons any flavor preserves and
  2 tablespoons finely chopped peanuts

In each case, beat combined ingredients until blended. Serve immediately or cover and refrigerate. Use on toast, hot breads, pancakes, waffles, coffeecakes or to make finger sandwiches.

Soufflé Silver Dollars

Serve these delectable little puffs for brunch, or as dessert after a light meal.

Strawberry-Brandy Butter, see below
1/4 cup biscuit mix
1 tablespoon sugar

1/4 cup dairy sour cream
4 eggs, separated

Prepare Strawberry-Brandy Butter. Preheat griddle according to manufacturer's directions to 375F (190C). Stir together biscuit mix, sugar, sour cream and egg yolks until blended. Beat egg whites until stiff but not dry. Stir half of beaten egg whites into batter, then fold in remaining egg whites. Lightly grease griddle. Spoon on batter, using about 1 tablespoon for each cake. Spread batter gently so cakes will be round. Cook until 1 or 2 bubbles appear on surface and undersides are delicately browned, 30 to 45 seconds. Turn and brown other sides. Lift to heated serving plates; do not stack, or pancakes will flatten. Top with Strawberry-Brandy Butter; serve immediately. Makes about 24 pancakes or 4 servings.

Strawberry-Brandy Butter   Photo on page 121.

Perfect for little dessert pancakes, but also good on scones or popovers.

3 tablespoons strawberry preserves
1-1/2 tablespoons cherry or other brandy
1/2 cup Home-Whipped Butter, page 111,
  made with unsalted butter,
  or commercial unsalted whipped butter
  or margarine

1/4 cup finely chopped blanched almonds

Place preserves and brandy in blender. Process at medium speed until well blended. Add butter or margarine. Process until blended and light. By hand, stir in almonds. Serve immediately or cover and refrigerate. Makes about 2/3 cup.

Toffee Butter

Spread on toast or toasted muffins, or try as a topping for hot cereal.

1/2 cup butter or margarine,
  room temperature
1/4 cup packed light-brown sugar

1/8 teaspoon ground cinnamon
1/2 teaspoon vanilla extract

In a small bowl, cream butter or margarine until fluffy. Add sugar and cream until light. Gently stir in cinnamon and vanilla. Serve immediately or cover and refrigerate. Makes about 2/3 cup.

Spicy Breakfast Bread

The glorious aroma as this bakes will have the family lined up ahead of time.

Sweet Lime Butter, see below
2 cups all-purpose flour
1 teaspoon baking powder
1 teaspoon baking soda
1 teaspoon ground cinnamon
1/4 teaspoon salt
1/4 teaspoon ground allspice
1/4 teaspoon ground cardamom

1/3 cup packed light-brown sugar
3/4 cup dairy sour cream
1/2 cup molasses
1/4 cup milk
1 egg
2 tablespoons butter or margarine, melted
Powdered sugar

Prepare and refrigerate Sweet Lime Butter. Preheat oven to 350F (175C). Butter and flour a 9" x 5" loaf pan; set aside. In a large bowl, combine flour, baking powder, baking soda, cinnamon, salt, allspice, cardamom and brown sugar. With a slotted spoon, stir until blended. In a medium bowl, beat together sour cream, molasses, milk, egg and butter or margarine. Stir into dry ingredients until blended. Pour into prepared pan. Bake in preheated oven until bread begins to pull away from side of pan and center springs back when lightly touched with your fingertip, 35 to 40 minutes. Let stand in pan 10 minutes, then turn out onto a serving plate. Sprinkle lightly with powdered sugar. Cut in slices and serve immediately. Pass Sweet Lime Butter to spread on bread. Makes about 8 servings.

Sweet Lime Butter

Best with fruited breads such as banana, orange or cranberry.

3/4 cup Home-Whipped Butter, page 111, made with unsalted butter, or commercial unsalted whipped butter or margarine, room temperature

2 teaspoons grated lime peel
3 tablespoons sifted powdered sugar
2 teaspoons lime juice

In a small bowl, beat together butter or margarine, lime peel and powdered sugar until fluffy. Stir in lime juice until blended. Serve immediately or cover and refrigerate. Remove from refrigerator 20 minutes before serving. Makes about 3/4 cup.

Orange-Honey Butter

For toast, popovers, muffins, flapjacks—any hot bread you can think of.

1/2 cup Home-Whipped Butter, page 111, or margarine, room temperature
3 tablespoons honey

1 tablespoon frozen orange-juice concentrate, thawed
1 teaspoon grated orange peel

In a small bowl, beat butter or margarine and honey until fluffy and light. Stir in orange-juice concentrate and orange peel. Serve immediately or cover and refrigerate. Makes about 2/3 cup.

Spicy Breakfast Bread with Strawberry-Brandy Butter, page 119, Sweet Lime Butter and Orange-Honey Butter. Garlic blossoms in background.

Herb & Spice Compounds

Apple-pie spice. Seasoned salt. Crab boil. Mixed pickling spices. *Fines herbes.* Poultry seasoning. Salad herbs. Curry powder. Chili powder. Chinese five-spice. *Bouquet garni.* Cinnamon sugar. These are only a few of the spice and herb compounds you'll find on supermarket shelves and in food specialty shops. They are rich in flavor and give authentic taste to anything from country-style foods to exotic dishes. They are also versatile, lending unusual flavor combinations to foods.

Commercial seasoning blends are considerably more expensive than individual spices and variety is limited. At home you can vary the flavoring elements to suit your own taste. Add a bit more cinnamon, cut down on the amount of tarragon or omit salt entirely for low-sodium diets.

Before you embark on a round of compounding seasonings at home, observe these few words of caution. In this one instance, fresh is not best. *Only dried herbs work well in these mixtures.* Citrus peels must also be dried for use in the formulas given in this section.

Store your finished products in jars with tight-fitting screwtop lids in a cool, dark, dry place. A few must be stored in the refrigerator.

In the pages that follow, you'll find a number of spice and herb blends to make at home, plus some inventive recipes that use them. The first time you prepare these compounds, follow the recipe carefully. The next time experiment a little until you get exactly the seasoning you want.

Menu

Winter After-Skating Warmup

Hot Buttered Rum
Hot Milk Punch
Portuguese Supper Soup, page 127
Dill-Seed Cottage Loaf, page 36
Home-Whipped Butter, page 111
Swedish Stuffed-Egg Salad, page 40
Cici Salad Sicilian-Style, page 24
Heavenly Devil's Food, page 80
Hot Coffee

Feast for a Dozen Curry-Lovers

Invite friends to join you for an authentic, wonderfully satisfying East-Indian meal.

Red-Radish Relish, page 148
Midsummer Chutney, page 145
Wilted Cucumbers, see below
2 tablespoons Calcutta Curry Blend,
 page 130
2 tablespoons vegetable oil
5 lbs. boneless lean lamb, cut in cubes
2 large onions, chopped
2 garlic cloves, minced
Hot water
1 tablespoon lemon juice

2 cups thinly sliced celery
Salt and ground black pepper to taste
2 Golden Delicious apples, peeled, diced
1/4 cup all-purpose flour
2 cups plain yogurt
2 tablespoons butter or margarine
6 large partially green bananas, thickly sliced
About 1/8 teaspoon ground cinnamon
Sambals, see below
8 cups hot cooked white rice
8 pita breads, split, toasted, buttered

Wilted Cucumbers:
3 large cucumbers, thinly sliced
Salt
1/2 teaspoon ground white pepper
1 teaspoon sugar

1/2 cup white-wine vinegar
1/4 cup vegetable oil
3 tablespoons snipped fresh or
 freeze-dried chives

Sambals:
2 cups coarsely chopped salted peanuts
6 hard-cooked eggs, chopped
15 green onions, thinly sliced
2 cups flaked unsweetened coconut

2 cups chopped seeded peeled tomatoes
2 cups julienne strips of
 green bell peppers
1 cup golden raisins

Prepare and refrigerate Red-Radish Relish, Midsummer Chutney and Wilted Cucumbers. Prepare Calcutta Curry Blend. All can be made at least a day in advance. Heat oil in a Dutch oven over medium heat. Add lamb; cook until lightly browned. Drain off fat. Add onions and garlic to skillet. Pour in enough hot water to cover lamb. Bring to a boil over medium-high heat; cover. Reduce heat. Simmer until tender, about 1-1/2 hours. Add lemon juice, celery and salt and pepper to taste. Simmer 10 minutes. Add apples. Simmer 5 minutes longer. In a small bowl, combine flour, yogurt and 2 tablespoons Calcutta Curry Blend, making a smooth paste. Stir into lamb mixture. Stirring constantly, cook until mixture bubbles and thickens. Melt butter or margarine in a large skillet over medium heat. Add banana slices. Sauté until lightly browned on all sides, about 3 minutes. Sprinkle lightly with cinnamon. Taste lamb mixture and add salt and pepper to taste. Add more Calcutta Curry Blend if a stronger flavor is desired. Keep mixture warm. Prepare Sambals. Spoon rice onto a large hot platter. Spoon lamb mixture over rice. Arrange dishes of Sambals, Wilted Cucumbers, Red-Radish Relish, Midsummer Chutney and browned bananas around platter of lamb mixture. Let diners serve themselves from platter, topping lamb mixture with their choice from other dishes. Serve with pita bread. Makes 12 servings.

Wilted Cucumbers:
Layer cucumbers in a large bowl, liberally salting each layer. Place a plate on top of cucumbers; weight down with heavy cans. Let stand at room temperature 2 hours. Pour into a colander. Rinse with cold water; drain. Combine white pepper, sugar, vinegar and oil. Spoon cucumbers into a serving dish. Add oil mixture; toss. Sprinkle with chives. Cover; refrigerate up to 24 hours.

Sambals:
Place each ingredient in a separate small dish.

On following pages: Feast for a Dozen Curry-Lovers. Wilted Cucumbers surround Red-Radish Relish, page 148.

Fines Herbes

Perfect in omelets, scrambled eggs, and to perk up dressings and sauces.

3 tablespoons dried leaf thyme
3 tablespoons dried leaf basil
3 tablespoons dried leaf savory

3 tablespoons dried grated lemon peel
3 tablespoons dried leaf marjoram
3 tablespoons dried rubbed sage

In a small bowl, blend all ingredients. Spoon into a screwtop jar. Cover tightly and store in a cool dry place. Makes about 1 cup.

Portuguese Seasoning

Use in hearty soups and in braising liquid for beef or pork.

3 (3-inch) cinnamon sticks
1/4 cup anise seeds

2 tablespoons whole cloves
2 tablespoons black peppercorns

Preheat oven to 300F (150C). Break each cinnamon stick into several pieces. Spread all ingredients in a large flat pan. Bake until crisp, about 30 minutes. In blender or spice grinder, process or grind mixture to make a fine powder. Cool to room temperature. Spoon into a screwtop jar. Cover tightly and store in a cool dry place. Makes about 3/4 cup.

Chinese Five-Spice Seasoning

Use sparingly to flavor chicken dishes; goes well with pork and fish, too.

1/4 cup ground ginger
2 tablespoons ground cinnamon
1 tablespoon ground allspice

1 tablespoon crushed anise seeds
1-1/2 teaspoons ground cloves

In a screwtop jar, combine all ingredients. Cover tightly and shake well. Store in a cool dry place. Makes about 1/2 cup.

Creole Seasoning

Just right for shrimp, crab and lobster, but good with any kind of fish.

8 teaspoons non-iodized salt
2 tablespoons ground black pepper
2 tablespoons garlic powder
8 teaspoons sweet paprika

8 teaspoons red (cayenne) pepper
4-1/2 teaspoons onion powder
1 tablespoon dried leaf thyme, crumbled
2 tablespoons dried grated lemon peel

In a small bowl, combine all ingredients. Spoon into a screwtop jar. Cover tightly and store in a cool dry place. Makes about 3/4 cup.

Portuguese Supper Soup

With bread and a salad, a meal in itself—one with an unforgettable flavor.

2 cups dried red beans	**About 1 qt. water**
1 teaspoon Portuguese Seasoning, page 126	**Salt**
3 ham shanks	**1 (8-oz.) can tomato sauce**
1 (1- to 1-1/2-lb.) sausage	**2 tablespoons vegetable oil**
(Portuguese linguiça, Mexican chorizo,	**1 medium onion, sliced**
Polish kielbasa or	**2 tablespoons snipped fresh parsley**
American smoked farm-style)	**2 large potatoes, peeled, diced**
1 small beef soup bone	

Rinse and pick over beans. Place in a medium bowl. Add cold water to cover. Let stand at room temperature overnight. Prepare Portuguese Seasoning; set aside. In a large pot, combine ham shanks, sausage, soup bone and 1 quart water. Bring to a boil over high heat; cover. Reduce heat to low. Simmer 1 hour. Stir in 1 teaspoon salt, tomato sauce, Portuguese Seasoning and 2 cups water. Drain soaked beans. Add to meat mixture. Bring back to a boil over high heat; cover. Reduce heat to low. Simmer 1 hour longer, adding more water if necessary. In a medium skillet, heat oil over medium heat. Add onion and parsley. Sauté until onion is almost tender. Add to soup with potatoes. Continue to simmer until meat, beans and potatoes are tender, about 30 minutes. Remove soup bone. Cut off meat; add meat to pot, discarding bone. Remove ham shanks. Cut off meat and return to pot, discarding bones and skin. Remove sausage. Cut into thick slices and return to pot. Season to taste with salt. Simmer 10 minutes. Serve at once, or cool, refrigerate, and reheat before serving. Makes 8 main-dish servings.

Seasoned Salts & Peppers

Seasoned Salt I
3/4 cup coarse kosher salt
4-1/2 teaspoons onion powder
2-1/4 teaspoons dry mustard
1-1/2 teaspoons ground celery seeds
3/4 teaspoon sweet or half-sweet paprika
1/4 teaspoon red (cayenne) pepper
1/4 teaspoon chili powder
1/4 teaspoon ground turmeric

Seasoned Salt II
1/2 cup coarse sea salt
1/4 cup granular kelp
1 teaspoon garlic powder
1 tablespoon dried leaf basil
1 teaspoon white peppercorns

Seasoned Pepper I
1/4 cup black peppercorns
2 tablespoons white peppercorns
1 teaspoon crushed dried red-pepper flakes

Seasoned Pepper II
6 tablespoons white peppercorns
2 tablespoons dried grated lemon peel
2 tablespoons dried parsley flakes

In blender, process ingredients for each salt or pepper at medium speed until mixture reaches desired fineness. Spoon into a screwtop jar. Cover tightly and store in a cool dry place. Serve as you would serve plain salt or pepper.

Spaghetti Squash Italian-Style

Use the sauce with any pasta; use either of the seasonings in green salads and casseroles.

1 (about 2-1/2-lb.) spaghetti squash
1/4 cup Northern Italian or
   Southern Italian Seasoning, see below
4 medium tomatoes, diced
2 tablespoons olive oil
1/4 cup dry red wine or mixture of
   2 tablespoons red-wine vinegar and
   2 tablespoons water

1 (4-oz.) can mushroom pieces and stems,
   undrained
1 teaspoon sugar
3/4 teaspoon salt

Cut squash in half lengthwise. Spoon out and discard seeds. Pour water 1 inch deep in a 12-inch skillet. Bring to a boil over high heat. Place squash, cut-side down, in boiling water. Cover skillet. Reduce heat to low. Simmer until tender, about 40 minutes. Prepare Northern or Southern Italian Seasoning. In a medium saucepan, combine tomatoes and oil. Place over medium heat. Sauté 3 minutes, stirring frequently. Add wine or vinegar-water mixture. Add mushrooms with liquid, sugar and salt. Reduce heat to low. Stirring occasionally, simmer 5 minutes. Gently stir in 1/4 cup Italian seasoning. Simmer 10 minutes longer. Place cooked squash, cut-side down, on paper towels to drain, 3 or 4 minutes. With 2 forks, remove spaghetti-like strings from squash. Arrange on a hot platter. Spoon sauce over squash. Serve immediately. Makes 4 to 6 servings.

Italian Seasonings

Choose your favorite to give a touch of Italy to any pasta dish.

Northern Italian Seasoning:
3/4 cup grated Romano cheese (2-1/4 oz.)
1 tablespoon dried minced garlic
1 tablespoon dried parsley flakes

2 teaspoons dried leaf basil
1/2 teaspoon dried leaf thyme
1/8 teaspoon red (cayenne) pepper

Southern Italian Seasoning:
3/4 cup grated Parmesan Cheese (2-1/4 oz.)
1/2 cup dried parsley flakes
3 tablespoons dried minced onion
1 tablespoon dried leaf oregano

1 teaspoon dried minced garlic
1 teaspoon dried red-pepper flakes
1/8 teaspoon ground cloves

In a small bowl, combine all ingredients for either mix. Stir to blend. Spoon into a screwtop jar. Cover tightly and store in refrigerator. Use within 4 to 6 weeks. Each mix makes about 1 cup.

How to Make Spaghetti Squash Italian-Style

1/Cook and drain squash. Use 2 forks to remove spaghetti-like strings from squash.

2/Arrange spaghetti squash on a platter. Spoon sauce over squash.

Daria's Chicken Chili

Also season eggs, beef-and-bean chili, and cheese dishes with Daria's Chili Powder.

**1 tablespoon Daria's Chili Powder,
  page 131**
12 chicken thighs
1-1/2 cups hot water
1 medium onion, sliced

2 celery stalks, cut in thin diagonal slices
1 (6-oz.) can tomato paste
1/3 cup quartered pitted ripe olives
3 cups hot cooked white rice

Prepare Daria's Chili Powder; set aside. Place chicken thighs in a large, heavy skillet; add water. Bring to a boil over medium-high heat. Reduce heat to low. Simmer, uncovered, 15 minutes. With a slotted spoon, place chicken in a single layer on a large plate or platter. Add onion and celery to liquid in skillet. Continue to simmer until tender and liquid is reduced to about 1 cup. When chicken is cool enough to handle, remove skin. Cut skin into small pieces. Remove meat from bone. Cut chicken meat into large dice; set aside. Add skin, tomato paste and 1 tablespoon Daria's Chili Powder to skillet; stir. Stir in diced chicken. Stirring frequently, simmer, uncovered, 20 minutes. Stir in olives. Spoon over hot rice. Makes 6 servings.

Broiled Fillets Creole-Style

Use this zesty seasoning to highlight any fish or shellfish dish.

1-1/2 lbs. sole or haddock fillets,
  fresh or frozen
1 tablespoon Creole Seasoning, page 126
1/2 cup butter or margarine, melted

1 (4- to 6-oz.) can tiny shrimp, drained
1/4 lb. mushrooms, coarsely chopped
2 tablespoons snipped fresh parsley

If fish is frozen, thaw enough to separate fillets. Prepare Creole Seasoning. Pat fish dry with paper towels. In a small saucepan, stir 1 tablespoon Creole Seasoning into melted butter or margarine. Preheat broiler if manufacturer directs. Lightly grease broiler pan. Place fillets on pan. Brush with seasoning mixture. Broil 2 to 3 inches from source of heat, without turning, until fish is opaque and flakes readily, 2 to 5 minutes. Brush again with seasoning mixture about halfway through broiling period. Place fish on a hot platter; keep warm. Add shrimp, mushrooms and parsley to remaining seasoning mixture. Pour in juices left in pan from cooking fish. Bring to boiling point. Pour over fish. Serve immediately. Makes 4 to 6 servings.

Pork Seasoning Mix

Points up the rich flavor of pork chops, roasts and braised dishes.

1/2 cup dried grated orange peel
2 teaspoons onion powder
2 teaspoons dried rubbed sage
1 teaspoon dried leaf thyme

1 teaspoon salt
1 teaspoon celery salt
1/2 teaspoon coarsely ground black pepper

Combine all ingredients in a screwtop jar. Cover tightly and shake well. Store in a cool dry place. Shake again before measuring. Makes about 3/4 cup.

To Use
To season meat that will not be breaded, combine 1 tablespoon Pork Seasoning Mix with 2 teaspoons vegetable oil. Rub mixture well into meat. Let stand 20 minutes at room temperature before cooking.

Calcutta Curry Blend

Use in beef, lamb, poultry, fish and vegetable curries, and in salads.

12 cardamom pods
2 tablespoons coriander seeds
1-1/2 teaspoons cumin seeds
1 tablespoon ground turmeric
1 tablespoon ground ginger

1 tablespoon whole fenugreek, if desired
1-1/2 teaspoons ground allspice
1-1/2 teaspoons ground cinnamon
1-1/2 teaspoons ground white pepper
1-1/2 teaspoons ground cloves

Remove cardamom seeds from pods; discard pods. Place cardamon seeds and remaining ingredients in a mortar or heavy bowl. With pestle or back of a heavy spoon, crush ingredients until powdery, with no distinguishable pieces. Spoon into a screwtop jar. Cover tightly and store in a cool dry place. Makes about 1/2 cup.

Perfect Seasoned Rice

These delicious mixes lend a personal touch to rice.

2 tablespoons Curry, Beef-Onion or Chicken-Herb Rice Seasoning Mix, see below	**1 cup uncooked long-grain white rice**
2 tablespoons butter or margarine	**2 teaspoons salt**
	2 cups water

Curry Rice Seasoning Mix:

1/2 cup instant chicken-flavor bouillon powder or granules	**1 teaspoon ground turmeric**
2 teaspoons curry powder	**1/2 teaspoon dried grated lemon peel**

Beef-Onion Rice Seasoning Mix:

1/2 cup instant beef-flavor bouillon powder or granules	**1/2 teaspoon celery salt**
2 tablespoons dried minced onion	**1/2 teaspoon white pepper**

Chicken-Herb Rice Seasoning Mix:

1/2 cup instant chicken-flavor bouillon powder or granules	**1 tablespoon dried leaf basil, crumbled**
1/2 cup dried parsley flakes	**1 tablespoon dried leaf thyme, crumbled**
1 tablespoon dried minced onion	**1 teaspoon garlic powder**

Prepare rice seasoning mix of your choice. In a medium saucepan, melt butter or margarine. Add rice. Stirring constantly, sauté until translucent but not browned, about 2 minutes. Stir in salt, water and 2 tablespoons rice seasoning mix. Bring to a boil over medium-high heat; cover. Reduce heat. Simmer until rice is tender, about 20 minutes. Fluff with a fork. Serve immediately. Makes 4 servings.

Rice Seasoning Mixes:
In separate screwtop jars, combine ingredients for each of the mixes. Cover tightly and shake well. Label jars with contents. Store in a cool dry place.

Daria's Chili Powder

Goes beyond traditional chili to season eggs, poultry, beef and lamb.

4 large dried mild chili peppers	**1/2 teaspoon whole allspice**
2 medium dried hot chili peppers	**1/4 cup dried leaf oregano**
4 teaspoons cumin seeds	**2 tablespoons garlic powder**
1/2 teaspoon whole cloves	**1 tablespoon salt**
1 teaspoon coriander seeds	**1/2 teaspoon sugar**

Remove stems and seeds from peppers. Cut peppers into small pieces. Place in a heavy skillet. Add cumin, cloves, coriander and allspice. Stir constantly over low heat until mixture begins to crackle and gives off aroma of peppers. Cool to room temperature. Grind pepper mixture in blender with oregano, garlic powder, salt and sugar until mixture becomes a fine powder. Spoon into a screwtop jar. Cover tightly and store in a cool dry place. Makes about 1 cup.

How to Make Bouquet Garni

1/Place ingredients in center of each cheesecloth square.

2/Bring edges of each square together. Tie securely with string.

Hungarian Hunter's Soup

Use the Hungarian Goulash Spices to season other soups, stews and casseroles.

1-1/2 lbs. beef round
2 tablespoons vegetable oil
3 cups Beef Stock, page 98,
   or canned beef broth
2 cups water
1 large onion, thinly sliced
1 tablespoon Hungarian Goulash Spices,
   opposite page

1 cup dry red wine
1 lb. sauerkraut, rinsed, drained
Salt and ground black pepper
Dairy sour cream
Sweet paprika

Trim fat from beef. Cut beef into 1/2-inch cubes. Heat oil in a large saucepan or pot. Add beef cubes. Cook over medium heat until browned on all sides. Add stock or broth, water and onion. Bring to a boil over high heat; cover. Reduce heat to low. Simmer until beef is tender, about 1 hour. Prepare Hungarian Goulash Spices. Add wine, sauerkraut and 1 tablespoon Hungarian Goulash Spices to soup and stir. Simmer, covered, 30 minutes. Season to taste with salt and pepper. Simmer 5 minutes longer. Top each serving with a dollop of sour cream. Sprinkle paprika over sour cream. Makes 6 servings.

Bouquet Garni

Simmer in soups, stews, or any sort of braised poultry or meat dish.

8 garlic cloves, peeled
1/2 cup dried parsley flakes
8 teaspoons dried leaf basil
8 teaspoons dried leaf rosemary

8 teaspoons dried leaf oregano
16 bay leaves
48 black peppercorns

Cut eight 3-inch squares from double-thick cheesecloth. Lay squares out on a flat surface. Into center of each, place 1 garlic clove, 1 tablespoon parsley, 1 teaspoon each of basil, rosemary and oregano, 2 bay leaves and 6 peppercorns. Bring edges of each cheesecloth square together to form a bag. Tie securely with white cotton string. Place in a screwtop jar. Cover tightly and store in a cool dry place. Makes 8 Bouquets Garni.

Savory Braised Lamb Shanks

For sublime flavor, drop a Bouquet Garni into the pot with any simmering meat or poultry.

1 Bouquet Garni, see above
2 tablespoons vegetable oil
4 whole lamb shanks
1 teaspoon salt

1/2 cup chopped onion
1-1/2 cups hot water
1/2 cup chopped pecans
2 cups hot cooked brown rice

Prepare Bouquet Garni; set aside. In a large heavy skillet with a lid, heat oil over medium heat. Add lamb shanks. Brown on all sides. Remove lamb. Pour off fat from skillet. Return lamb to skillet. Sprinkle with salt. Add onion and hot water. Place Bouquet Garni in water. Bring to a boil; cover. Reduce heat. Simmer until lamb is tender, 1-1/2 to 2 hours. In a medium bowl, gently stir pecans into hot rice. Mound in center of a hot platter. Arrange lamb shanks around rice; keep warm. Boil liquid in skillet over high heat until reduced to about 3/4 cup. Discard Bouquet Garni. Spoon liquid over shanks and rice. Serve immediately. Makes 4 servings.

Hungarian Goulash Spices

Good also in cabbage-family dishes such as broccoli and Brussels sprouts.

1/4 cup dried grated lemon peel
2 tablespoons garlic powder
1-1/2 tablespoons caraway seeds

2 teaspoons dried leaf thyme, crumbled
2 bay leaves, finely crumbled
2 tablespoons sweet paprika

In a screwtop jar, combine all ingredients. Cover tightly and store in a cool dry place. Makes about 2/3 cup.

Country-Style Pumpkin Pie

Use the spice blend in apple and peach pies, apple and rhubarb sauces.

**1 tablespoon Country Pumpkin-Pie Spice,
  see below**
4 eggs
1 (9-inch) pastry shell, unbaked

1 (16-oz.) can pumpkin
3/4 cup sugar
1/4 teaspoon salt
1-1/4 cups evaporated milk

Prepare Country Pumpkin-Pie Spice. Preheat oven to 450F (230C). In a large bowl, combine 3 whole eggs and yolk of fourth egg. Place white of fourth egg in pastry shell. Using your fingers, spread egg white over bottom and up side of shell. Beat eggs in bowl until whites and yolks are blended. Add pumpkin and sugar, beat well. Beat in 1 tablespoon Country Pumpkin-Pie Spice and salt. Gradually stir in evaporated milk until blended. Pour into prepared pie shell. Bake 10 minutes. Reduce heat to 350F (175C). Continue baking until a knife inserted halfway between center and edge of pie comes out clean, 40 to 50 minutes. Cool on a rack 20 minutes. Refrigerate until serving time. Makes 1 pie or 6 to 8 servings.

Country Pumpkin-Pie Spice

Great to flavor almost any fruit or berry pie—use to brighten fruit sauces, too.

1/4 cup dried grated orange peel
1/4 cup ground cinnamon
1 tablespoon ground nutmeg

1 tablespoon ground ginger
1 teaspoon ground cloves

In a small bowl, blend all ingredients. Spoon into a screwtop jar. Cover tightly and store in a cool dry place. Makes about 2/3 cup.

Five-Spice Baking Blend

Cookies, cakes and pies made with this will fill the house with heavenly aromas.

1/4 cup ground ginger
3 tablespoons ground cinnamon
2 tablespoons ground allspice

1 tablespoon ground nutmeg
1-1/2 teaspoons ground cloves

In a small bowl, combine all ingredients. Spoon into a screwtop jar. Cover tightly and store in a cool dry place. Makes about 2/3 cup.

To use: Add 1 tablespoon baking blend to cake and cookie batters and pie fillings.

Flavored Vinegars & Oils

A selection of flavorful vinegars and oils adds greatly to any cook's repertoire, lending subtle, enhanced flavors to a wide variety of dishes. They are available in some supermarkets or gourmet stores, or you can make your own.

Homemade flavored vinegars and oils are easy to make and have excellent keeping qualities. Vary them to suit your personal taste. Flavored vinegars include raisin, raspberry, strawberry, blueberry, lemon, lime, garlic, thyme and sage.

What do you start with? Basic vinegars begin with distilled white, cider, red- or white-wine vinegar. Add whatever fruit, vegetable, herb or spice you choose. Let the mixture stand long enough for the flavors to blend. If you like, try making your own wine vinegar. Use it in cooking, or as the base for a flavored vinegar.

Flavored or seasoned oils can easily be made. Combine basic salad oil, which is virtually without taste, plus a fruit, nut, vegetable, herb or spice. Let the mixture stand to extract and mingle the flavors.

Following are the instructions for making your own flavored vinegars and oils and using them in recipes. They will add immeasurably to your cooking enjoyment and expertise.

Menu

Country-Style Sunday Dinner

Red-Hot Jelly, page 150
Cream Cheese & Crackers
Cumberland Ham, page 89
Baked Sweet Potatoes
Polka Dot Slaw, page 141
Grandma Lauder's Crown Puddings, page 67
Hot Coffee
Milk for Children

Fresh Berry Vinegar

Use in dressing for fruit salads or brush over poultry to be grilled.

**6 cups fresh raspberries or hulled,
    halved strawberries**

**1 qt. white-wine vinegar
4 cups sugar**

Wash five 1-pint canning jars or bottles in hot soapy water; rinse. Sterilize by filling with boiling water. Drain just before filling. Scald lids or corks in boiling water. Place berries in a 3-quart glass or pottery bowl. Use potato masher to crush berries thoroughly. Stir in vinegar. Cover tightly and let stand 24 to 36 hours in a cool place. Place a strainer over a large enamel or stainless steel saucepan. Pour berry mixture through strainer, pressing with back of a spoon to extract as much pulp as possible. Add sugar; stir well. Place berry mixture over medium heat. Bring to a boil, stirring. Reduce heat to low. Stirring constantly, simmer 5 minutes. Pour into prepared jars or bottles. Attach lids or corks. Invert canning jars 5 to 10 seconds, then stand upright to cool. Cool to room temperature. Label and date. Store in refrigerator; use within 3 months. Makes 5 pints.

Lemon-Mint Vinegar

Perfect in dressings for seafood or poultry salads and in marinades.

**1 (1/4-inch wide) spiral of
    lemon peel**

**4 long fresh mint sprigs
3-3/4 cups white-wine vinegar**

To make a spiral of lemon peel, use a swivel-blade vegetable peeler or citrus stripper. Peel or cut a long, 1/4-inch wide strip of lemon peel. Wash a 1-quart bottle or jar in hot soapy water, rinse. Sterilize by filling with boiling water. Let stand 10 minutes. Discard water. Scald lid or cork in boiling water. Place lemon peel and mint in sterile bottle or jar. Pour in vinegar. Cover tightly with sterile cork or jar lid. Label and date. Let stand in a warm, sunny place 10 days before using. Store in a cool dark dry place. Use within 6 months. Makes 1 quart.

Variation
Peel and split 3 garlic cloves. Add to bottle or jar before adding vinegar. Use in dressing for a romaine or endive salad, sprinkle over cottage cheese or use as a marinade for cooked shrimp.

Lime Vinegar

Cool and tart, perfect for fruit-salad dressings and light sauces.

**2 fresh limes
1 qt. white-wine vinegar**

Wash a 6-cup bottle in hot soapy water; rinse. Sterilize by filling with boiling water. Let stand 10 minutes. Discard water. Scald jar lid or cork in boiling water. Quarter limes. Thread quarters on a long bamboo skewer. Gently insert into sterile bottle. In a medium saucepan, bring vinegar to a simmer. Pour into bottle over lime quarters. Attach lid or cork. Label and date. Let stand in a cool dark dry place 10 days before using. Use within 6 months. Makes 1 quart.

Clockwise from top: Lemon-Mint Vinegar; Hot Herbed Vinegar, page 139; Rosemary in Olive Oil, see box on page 31; Lime Vinegar; Olivey Oil, page 140; Fresh Berry Vinegar made with Raspberries; Spicy Oil, page 141.

Seeded Vinegar

Use for a very special vinaigrette or rub into pork roasts or chops before cooking.

**2 tablespoons mustard, celery or
   caraway seeds**

1 qt. cider vinegar

Place seeds in a mortar and bruise gently with a pestle. Or, place in a small dish and crush with back of a heavy spoon; set aside. Wash a 1-quart canning jar in hot soapy water; rinse. Sterilize by filling with boiling water. Let stand at least 10 minutes. Heat vinegar in an enamel or stainless steel saucepan over low heat. Place seeds on center of a 5-inch square of cheesecloth. Gather edges of cheesecloth to form a bag. Tie with string, leaving 1 end of string about 10 inches long. Empty water from jar. Lower bag into jar until it is suspended about 1 inch above bottom of jar. Loop string around neck of jar; tie so bag can move freely within. Sterilize jar lid in boiling water. When vinegar begins to simmer, pour into jar. Attach lid. Label and date. Let stand in a cool dark place 10 days, moving cheesecloth bag up and down several times each day. After 10 days, remove and discard bag. Replace lid on jar. Store in a cool dark dry place. Use within 8 months. Makes 1 quart.

Fruited Vinegar

Fragrant, ruby-red and unbelievably delicious for many uses.

**2 (10-oz.) pkgs. frozen raspberries,
   thawed**

5-1/4 cups red-wine vinegar

Wash four 1-pint canning jars or bottles in hot soapy water; rinse. Sterilize in boiling water. Drain just before filling. Prepare lids as manufacturer directs. Drain raspberries, reserving juice to thicken and use as a sauce for ice cream or cake. Gently rinse raspberries with cold water; drain again. Place in a large enamel or stainless steel saucepan. Add vinegar. Let stand overnight, uncovered, at room temperature. Bring raspberry mixture to a boil over medium-high heat. Boil, uncovered, 3 minutes. Cool. Strain, discarding solids. Fill jars or bottles, close tightly. Label and date. Let stand 3 to 4 weeks at room temperature before using. Store in a cool dark dry place. Use within 4 months. Makes 4 pints.

Variations

Substitute frozen strawberries, blueberries or peaches for raspberries, using red-wine or white-wine vinegar, as desired. Or, use 3/4 cup golden raisins or finely diced, pitted prunes for unusual, delightful flavor.

How to Make Seeded Vinegar

1/With mortar and pestle or a small dish and back of a heavy spoon, gently bruise seeds.

2/Lower seed packet into jar to 1 inch from bottom. Loop string around neck of jar.

Hot Herbed Vinegar   Photo on page 137.

For any strong-flavored meat or vegetable—but be careful, it can burn!

5 hot chili peppers, fresh or dried
1 bay leaf
4 fresh coriander (cilantro) sprigs

4 fresh sage sprigs
2 fresh rosemary sprigs
3-3/4 cups red-wine vinegar

Wash a 1-quart glass jar in hot soapy water; rinse. Sterilize by filling with boiling water. Let stand 10 minutes. Discard water. In sterile jar, combine chili peppers, bay leaf, coriander, sage and rosemary. In an enamel or stainless-steel saucepan, bring vinegar to a boil. Pour into jar. Leave uncovered while mixture cools. Scald jar lid in boiling water. Attach lid to jar. Label and date. Store in a cool dark dry place at least 7 days before using. Use within 8 months. Makes about 1 quart.

Homemade Wine Vinegar

Time and patience are the extra ingredients for a fine vinegar.

1 cup red-wine vinegar
1 cup dry red wine

2 cups dry white wine
3 sprigs fresh thyme, if desired

Wash a 1-quart cask, crock or bottle in hot soapy water; rinse. Sterilize by filling with boiling water. Let stand 10 minutes. Discard water. Pour wine vinegar into sterile container. Add red and white wines. Cover with cheesecloth to permit air circulation and keep vinegar clean. Let stand about 3 months at about 70F (20C). Sterilize two 1-pint bottles or jars. Scald caps, lids or corks in boiling water. Place thyme sprigs in 1 jar, if desired. Pour aged homemade wine vinegar into bottles or jars. Cover tightly with corks or jar lids. Label and date. Store in a cool dark dry place. Use within 8 months. Makes 2 pints.

Variations

Tarragon or Rosemary Vinegar: Substitute fresh tarragon or rosemary sprigs for thyme.
Vinaigre de Vin Rouge: Substitute 2 cups additional dry red wine for white wine.
Vinaigre de Vin Blanc: Substitute white-wine vinegar for red-wine vinegar and 1 cup additional dry white wine for red wine.

Olive-Garlic Oil

Use in any recipe where both olive oil and garlic are included.

16 small Italian-cured or
 Greek-cured ripe olives

16 large garlic cloves, peeled, halved
1 qt. olive oil

Place olives and garlic in a shallow glass or pottery bowl. Pour in olive oil. Cover and let stand in a cool dark dry place 10 days, stirring once each day. Wash a 1-quart bottle or jar in hot soapy water; rinse. Sterilize by filling with boiling water. Let stand 10 minutes. Discard water. Scald lid or cork in boiling water. Strain oil into sterile bottle or jar. Attach lid or cork. Label and date. Store in a cool dark dry place. Use within 2 months. Drain garlic and olives on paper towels; use in salads. Makes 1 quart.

Olivey Oil   Photo on page 137.

A delicious, easy-on-the-pocketbook substitute for true olive oil.

12 unpitted, brine-packed green olives
2 cups vegetable oil

Wash a 1-pint bottle or canning jar in hot soapy water; rinse. Sterilize by filling with boiling water. Let stand 10 minutes. Discard water. Scald lid or cork in boiling water. Place olives in sterile bottle or jar. Pour oil over olives. Attach lid or cork. Label and date. Let stand at room temperature 1 week before using. Store in a cool dark dry place. Use in any recipe that calls for olive oil. Use within 2 months. Makes 1 pint.

Spicy Oil   Photo on page 137.

Excellent in dressings for hearty vegetables and in marinades for beef and lamb.

12 whole coriander seeds, crushed
6 whole allspice
5 whole cloves
3 garlic cloves, peeled, halved

2 whole cinnamon sticks
1 small hot chili pepper
1 (1/4-inch) slice fresh gingerroot
1 qt. vegetable oil

Wash a 1-quart bottle or jar in hot soapy water; rinse. Sterilize by filling with boiling water. Let stand 10 minutes. Discard water. Scald lid or cork in boiling water. In sterile bottle or jar, combine coriander, allspice, cloves, garlic, cinnamon, pepper and gingerroot. Pour in oil almost to top of container. Attach lid or cork. Label and date. Let stand in a cool dark dry place at least 10 days before using. Use within 2 months. Makes 1 quart.

Tijuana Salad

Sprightly cousin of famous Caesar Salad—use the oil in other dressings, too.

3 hard-cooked eggs, shelled, halved
2/3 cup Olive-Garlic Oil, page 140
1/2 teaspoon salt
1/8 teaspoon red (cayenne) pepper
3 slices firm white bread, crusts trimmed

3 tablespoons red-wine vinegar
8 cups mixed salad greens,
  in bite-size pieces
3/4 cup shredded Swiss cheese (3 oz.)

Coarsely chop egg whites; set aside. Place egg yolks in bottom of a 3-quart salad bowl. Mash yolks with a fork until smooth. Pour 3 tablespoons Olive-Garlic Oil into a large heavy skillet; set aside. Slowly add remaining oil to egg yolks, stirring with a fork until smooth. Stir in salt and red pepper. Place skillet with oil over medium heat. Cut bread slices 3 times across in each direction to produce small cubes. Toss and cook in oil until crisp and golden brown. Drain on paper towels. Stir vinegar into egg-yolk mixture. Add salad greens. Toss until coated. Add reserved egg whites, cheese and drained bread cubes. Toss again. Serve immediately. Makes 6 servings.

Polka-Dot Slaw

Good with pork or chicken dishes or as a relish on hamburgers or frankfurters.

4 cups finely shredded cabbage
1 cup shredded carrot
2 tablespoons grated onion
1/2 cup finely diced green bell pepper
1/3 cup vegetable oil

2 tablespoons whipping cream
3 tablespoons Seeded Vinegar, page 138,
  made with caraway seeds
1/2 teaspoon salt

In a medium bowl, toss cabbage, carrot, onion and pepper. In a small bowl, beat oil and cream with a rotary beater until blended. Beat in vinegar and salt. Pour over cabbage mixture; toss until coated. Serve immediately, or refrigerate up to 3 hours. Makes 6 servings.

Tart-Sweet Beef Pot Roast

This version of German sauerbraten makes a hearty cool-weather meal.

1 cup Hot Herbed Vinegar, page 139
2 cups water
1-1/2 teaspoons salt
4 lbs. beef rump roast or sirloin tip
2 medium onions, sliced

2 tablespoons vegetable oil
2 tablespoons all-purpose flour
5 tablespoons cold water
2 tablespoons minced candied ginger

In a medium saucepan, combine vinegar, 2 cups water and salt. Bring to a boil over medium-high heat. Remove from heat. Place meat in a glass or pottery bowl just large enough to accommodate it. Add onions. Pour hot vinegar mixture over meat and onions. Refrigerate 2 days, turning meat once each day. Remove meat from marinade. Pat dry with paper towels. Reserve onions in marinade. Heat oil in a 6-quart Dutch oven over medium-high heat. Add meat. Brown on all sides. Add marinade and onions. Bring to a boil. Reduce heat to low. Cover and simmer until meat is tender when pierced with a fork, about 3 hours. Place meat on a hot platter; keep hot. Mix flour with 5 tablespoons cold water to make a smooth thin paste. Increase heat to medium-high. Stirring vigorously, slowly add flour mixture to cooking liquid. Boil 1 minute, stirring constantly. Add ginger. Boil and stir 1 minute longer. Serve meat and gravy separately. Makes 8 servings.

Farm-Style Vinegar Pie

A luscious sweet-tart dessert, topped with a cloud of meringue.

1-1/3 cups sugar
3 tablespoons all-purpose flour
1/4 teaspoon salt
1/8 teaspoon ground nutmeg
2 tablespoons butter or margarine
1 cup water

3 tablespoons Lemon-Mint Vinegar,
   page 136
3 eggs, separated
1 (9-inch) pastry shell, baked, cooled
Lemon twists and mint leaves for garnish

In a small bowl, combine 1 cup sugar, flour, salt and nutmeg; set aside. In a medium saucepan, heat butter or margarine with water over low heat until melted. Add Lemon-Mint Vinegar. Stirring constantly, gradually add sugar mixture. Stirring frequently, cook over low heat until thickened. In a small bowl, beat egg yolks slightly. Beat in about 1/2 cup hot mixture. Stir egg-yolk mixture into hot mixture in pan. Cook 2 minutes, stirring constantly. Cool slightly. Spoon evenly into baked pastry shell. Preheat oven to 350F (175C). Beat egg whites until soft peaks form. Beat in remaining 1/3 cup sugar, 1 tablespoon at a time, until stiff but not dry. Spoon onto pie surface. Spread with a knife, so meringue touches crust all around edge. Bake in preheated oven until meringue is a delicate brown, about 12 minutes. Cool slightly, then refrigerate until ready to serve. Makes 8 servings.

All the vinegars and many oils used in recipes in this chapter can be replaced by commercial products.

Old-Fashioned Sponge Candy

An airy treat that may well come as a sweet surprise to the younger generation.

1 cup sugar
1/2 cup molasses
1/2 cup light corn syrup

1 tablespoon Lemon-Mint Vinegar, page 136
1 tablespoon baking soda

Generously butter a 9-inch square baking pan; set aside. In a large saucepan, combine sugar, molasses, corn syrup and vinegar. Cook over medium heat, stirring constantly, until sugar dissolves. Cover pan for 1 minute, to let steam wash down sugar crystals clinging to side of pan. Attach a candy thermometer to side of pan. Reduce heat to medium-low. Cook, without stirring, until sugar mixture reaches hard-crack stage, 300F (150C) on thermometer. Remove from heat. Stir in baking soda. Mixture will foam and increase in volume. Pour into prepared pan to cool. To serve, break into pieces by striking with the handle of a large knife. Store in an airtight metal container up to 3 weeks. Makes about 24 pieces.

How to Make Old-Fashioned Sponge Candy

1/Remove pan from heat; stir in soda. Mixture will foam and increase in volume.

2/To serve, break into pieces. Use a small wooden mallet or handle of a knife.

Condiments

The main dish is the heart of the meal and the dessert the grand finale. However, condiments, especially out-of-the-ordinary ones, give a meal individuality. Condiments are substances added to or served as accompaniments to food. They are usually tart or tart-sweet, distinctive and often pungent in flavor. Shelves of supermarkets and specialty food shops offer a wide variety: jams, jellies, pickles, chutneys, sauces, fruits and vegetables in many kinds of syrups.

With such variety available, why bother with homemade condiments? For many reasons. Store-bought condiments, especially the unusual ones, are generally expensive. Homemade quality tends to be higher, and the condiments made in your own kitchen contain no artificial flavors or preservatives. Homemade treats such as those you'll find in this section make great hostess or holiday gifts. Finally, you can prepare a number of delightful combinations at home that are not available in stores. And, if you enjoy cooking, there is always the adventure of producing a new treat.

If your kitchen time and energies are limited, be selective. Buy those condiments that are difficult or time-consuming. Make those, such as Spiced Currants, that are easy to prepare, and almost impossible to find in stores.

Most homemade condiments will keep well in the refrigerator one to four weeks. Some can be frozen three to six months. Almost all can be canned by the water-bath method for longer storage. Follow the manufacturer's instructions for preparing and sealing jars.

Menu

Teenager's Get-Together

Mugs of Turkish-Wtyle Lentil Soup, page 39
Choice-of-Butters Burgers, page 112
Onions Trafalgar Square, page 96
Sliced Currants, page 153
Red-Radish Relish, page 148
Hot-Snap-Bean Salad, page 24
Speculaas, page 21
Coconut-Cornflake Cookies, page 74
Ultimate Fudge Sundae, page 82
Assorted Soft Drinks

Midsummer Chutney

Perfect partner for roasted or broiled chicken, or for any curry dish.

2 lbs. nectarines
2 tablespoons grated lemon peel
1/3 cup lemon juice
1 small onion, finely chopped
1-1/4 cups packed light-brown sugar
1/2 cup cider vinegar

1/2 cup diced pitted prunes
1/4 cup minced candied ginger
2 teaspoons salt
1 teaspoon ground allspice
1/4 teaspoon ground cloves
3/4 teaspoon dry mustard

Halve and pit nectarines. Cut into 1/2-inch pieces. Place in a 4-quart saucepan. Add lemon peel, lemon juice, onion, sugar and vinegar. Bring to a boil over medium-high heat. Stir in remaining ingredients. Reduce heat to low. Stirring frequently, simmer, uncovered, until very thick, about 1 hour. Spoon into a container or jar with a tight-fitting lid. Cool. Cover and store in refrigerator up to 4 weeks. Makes 4 cups.

Greengage Chutney

Like the ant, be provident—make this in summer to store for next winter.

1 lb. light-brown sugar
2 cups distilled white vinegar
1/4 cup chopped candied ginger
1 garlic clove, minced
2 teaspoons ground cloves
2 teaspoons ground cinnamon
1/2 teaspoon ground nutmeg

1/4 teaspoon celery seeds
1 teaspoon salt
1/4 teaspoon red (cayenne) pepper
1 cup chopped onion
1 cup chopped green bell pepper
6 cups coarsely chopped greengage plums
   (about 2-1/2 lbs.)

Wash six 1/2-pint canning jars in hot soapy water; rinse. Keep hot until needed. Prepare 6 lids as manufacturer directs. In a large pot, combine sugar, vinegar, ginger, garlic, cloves, cinnamon, nutmeg, celery seeds, salt and red pepper. Stirring constantly, bring to a boil over medium-high heat. Add onions, green peppers and plums. Bring back to a boil. Reduce heat to medium-low. Cook until thickened, 20 minutes or more, stirring frequently to prevent burning. Fill and cover 1 jar at a time. Pour hot mixture to within 1/4 inch of jar rim. Release trapped air. Wipe rim of jar with a clean damp cloth. Attach lid. Place filled jars in hot water in water-bath canner. Cover all jars with hot water. Bring to a boil. Boil 15 minutes at sea level. Add 1 minute for each 1000 feet of altitude. Remove jars from canner; do not tighten lids. Cool on a rack or on towels in a place free from drafts. Press down on center of lid. If lid is down, seal is completed. If lid goes down as you press, remove ring and tip jar to side to see if there is leakage. Holding edge of lid with several fingers of 1 hand, lift jar 1 inch above table. If lid holds, seal is completed. Refrigerate jars that are not sealed. Label and store sealed jars in a cool dark place. Makes six 1/2-pint jars.

Variations

Substitute peeled peaches or other plums for greengage plums.

Memorable Rosemary Jelly

The flavor of this lovely-to-look-at jelly makes it a perfect complement to any lamb or veal roast.

4 or 5 sprigs fresh rosemary
3-1/4 cups sugar
1/2 cup orange juice

1/4 cup lime juice
3/4 cup water
1 (3-oz.) pouch liquid pectin

Sterilize three 6-ounce jelly glasses or other glasses. Wash rosemary. Snip off leaves and spread out to dry on paper towel. Snip dry leaves into small pieces. Measure 1-1/2 tablespoons. Reserve remaining leaves for another purpose. Using a mortar and pestle or a small container and the back of a heavy spoon, crush rosemary with 1/4 cup sugar. Place in a heavy 4-quart saucepan. Stir in orange juice, lime juice and water. Bring to a boil over medium-high heat. Reduce heat to low. Simmer 8 minutes. Increase heat to medium-high. Bring to a rolling boil. Stir in pectin. Stirring constantly, boil 30 seconds. Add remaining 3 cups sugar all at once. Stirring constantly, bring to a full, rolling boil that cannot be stirred down. Boil 1 minute, stirring constantly. Remove from heat. Let stand 1 minute. Skim off foam. Pour through a fine strainer into prepared glasses to within 1/4 inch of glass rim. Release trapped air. Wipe rim and inside of glasses down to jelly. Melt paraffin in a double boiler or over boiling water, never over direct heat. Remove paraffin from above boiling water and spoon a thin layer of paraffin into each glass. Let it harden. Spoon another layer of hot paraffin over the top. Tip glass slightly, rotating so paraffin runs against the side. Store in a cool dark place up to 6 months. Makes about three 6-ounce glasses.

Variations

Basil Jelly: Substitute 2 tablespoons snipped fresh basil, 1 cup tomato juice, 1/2 cup lemon juice and 1/4 cup water for rosemary, juices and water.

Lemon-Thyme Jelly: Substitute 1-1/2 tablespoons fresh lemon thyme, 1 cup dry red wine and 1/2 cup water for rosemary, juices and water.

Sweet Marjoram Jelly: Substitute 2 tablespoons snipped fresh sweet marjoram, 1 cup pineapple juice, 1/4 cup lime juice and 1/4 cup water for rosemary, juices and water.

Sage Jelly: Substitute 1 tablespoon snipped fresh sage, 1-1/4 cups dry red wine and 1/4 cup water for rosemary, juices and water.

French-Fried Walnuts

Use to garnish meat, poultry and fish salads, or serve as a snack with drinks.

4 cups shelled walnuts
1/2 cup sugar

Oil for deep-frying
Salt

In a large saucepan, bring 6 cups water to a boil. Add walnuts. Bring back to a boil. Cook 1 minute. Pour into a large strainer or colander. Rinse walnuts under running hot water. Drain well. In a large bowl, gently stir walnuts with sugar until sugar is dissolved. Let stand 5 minutes. Pour oil 2-1/2 inches deep into deep-fryer or a large saucepan. Heat oil to 375F (190C). Rinse and dry strainer or colander. Place over another large bowl; set aside. Using a slotted spoon, place walnuts, half at a time, in heated oil. Stirring frequently, fry until golden, about 5 minutes. Lift with slotted spoon and place in strainer or colander. Sprinkle lightly with salt; toss gently. Drain on paper towels. Cool completely. Place in an airtight plastic bag or jar. Nuts can be stored in refrigerator up to 3 weeks. Makes 4 cups.

Roast Veal San Francisco-Style, page 92, glazed with Memorable Rosemary Jelly, garnished with Spiced Apricots and Rosemary. Gravy and Cantaloupe Mustard, page 152, in background.

How to Make Hidden Farm Confetti Relish

1/Immerse tomatoes in hot water 30 seconds, then peel.

2/Cut kernels from blanched corn-on-the-cob.

Red-Radish Relish

Hearty flavor to accompany any beef dish, or to top off corned-beef sandwiches.

1 small onion, thinly sliced
2 cups thinly sliced small red radishes
1/4 cup minced green bell pepper
1/4 cup shredded carrot
2 tablespoons vegetable oil

1/2 cup cider vinegar
1 teaspoon salt
1-1/2 teaspoons sugar
1/4 teaspoon garlic juice
1/4 teaspoon coarsely ground black pepper

Separate onion slices into rings. In a medium bowl, combine onion rings, radishes, green pepper and carrot. Toss lightly. Pour oil into a small bowl. Stir in vinegar. Add salt, sugar, garlic juice and pepper. Stir vigorously to dissolve salt and sugar. Still stirring, pour over radish mixture. Cover and refrigerate 24 hours, stirring gently several times. Makes 2-3/4 cups.

Hidden Farm Confetti Relish

In the dead of winter this reminds you of a warm and sunny Indian summer.

12 large ripe tomatoes
12 large ears fresh corn, husked
8 green bell peppers
4 red bell peppers
1-1/2 cups chopped onions
1/4 cup celery seeds

2 tablespoons mustard seeds
1 tablespoon ground turmeric
3 tablespoons non-iodized salt
2 cups packed light-brown sugar
2 cups granulated sugar
1 qt. cider vinegar

Wash eight 1-pint canning jars in hot soapy water; rinse. Keep hot until needed. Prepare lids as manufacturer directs. Scald tomatoes in boiling water. Plunge into cold water. Quickly peel and cut into small pieces. Lower corn into boiling water. Boil 2 minutes. Rinse with cold water. Cut kernels from cobs. Remove stems, seeds and inner ribs from peppers. Cut peppers into small pieces. In a large pot, combine tomato pieces, corn kernels, pepper pieces, onions, celery and mustard seeds, turmeric, salt and sugars. Stir to blend. Stir in vinegar until blended. Bring to a boil over medium heat. Reduce heat to low. Simmer, uncovered, stirring frequently, until thick, 30 to 40 minutes. Fill only as many jars as will fit in your water-bath canner. Fill other jars just before processing. Pour hot mixture into 1 jar at a time to within 1/4 inch of jar rim. Release trapped air. Wipe rim of jars with a clean damp cloth. Place filled jars in hot water in water-bath canner. Cover all jars with hot water. Bring to a boil. Boil 10 minutes at sea level. Add 1 minute for each 1000 feet of altitude. Remove jars from canner; do not tighten lids. Cool on a rack or on towels in a place free from drafts. Press down on center of lids. If lid is down, seal is completed. If lid goes down as you press, remove ring and tip jar to side to see if there is leakage. Holding edge of lid with several fingers of 1 hand, lift jar 1 inch above table. If lid holds, seal is completed. Refrigerate jars that are not sealed. Label and store sealed jars in a cool dark place. Makes 8 pints.

Quick & Easy Fresh Relish

Good with hamburgers, hot dogs, any stir-fry or other Oriental dish.

2 cups finely grated white turnip
1 cup finely grated onion
1/2 cup white-wine vinegar

1/4 cup prepared horseradish
3 tablespoons sugar
3/4 teaspoon salt

In a large bowl, combine all ingredients. Stir to blend. Cover tightly and store in refrigerator up to 2 weeks. Makes about 3 cups.

If you don't have a water-bath canner, use a large pot that has a rack in the bottom. The jars should be on the rack, not touching each other. The pot must be deep enough so hot water can cover lids of jars and have room to boil at the top.

Red-Hot Jelly

Serve with beef or lamb, or to top crackers spread with cream cheese.

5 to 6 large red bell peppers
4 to 6 fresh hot red peppers
1 cup cider vinegar
5 cups sugar

1 (6-oz.) bottle or
  2 (3-oz.) pkgs. liquid pectin
5 drops red food coloring, if desired

Sterilize eight 6-ounce jelly glasses or other glasses and lids. Remove stems, seeds and inner ribs from peppers. Cut into small pieces. Keeping bell peppers and hot peppers separate, process in small batches in blender or food processor to make 1-3/4 cups pureed bell peppers and 1/4 cup pureed hot peppers. Combine pureed peppers in a large stainless-steel or glass-ceramic saucepan. Add vinegar and sugar. Stirring constantly, cook over high heat until sugar dissolves. Bring to a boil. Boil hard 4 minutes. Remove from heat. Stir in pectin. Bring to a full rolling boil that cannot be stirred down. Boil exactly 1 minute, stirring constantly. Stir in food coloring, if desired. Skim off foam. Ladle mixture into prepared glasses to within 1/4 inch of glass rim. Release trapped air; wipe rim and inside of glasses down to jelly. Melt paraffin in a double boiler or over boiling water, never over direct heat. Remove paraffin from above boiling water and spoon a thin layer of paraffin in each glass. Let it harden, 5 minutes. Spoon another layer of hot paraffin over the top. Tip glass slightly, rotating it all around, so paraffin runs against the side. Jelly can be stored in a cool dark place up to 6 months. Makes eight 6-ounce glasses.

Spicy Tomato Conserve

Make any time of year, using canned tomatoes for ease, speed and flavor.

3-1/2 cups packed light-brown sugar
1 teaspoon ground white pepper
2-1/2 cups distilled white vinegar
1 teaspoon ground cinnamon

2 cups chopped onions
1 teaspoon ground cloves
2 (28-oz.) cans tomatoes, with liquid
1 teaspoon salt

In a large pot, combine all ingredients. Cook and stir over medium heat until mixture comes to a boil. Reduce heat to low. Simmer, uncovered, until mixture is thick and dark brown in color, about 3 hours; stir frequently to prevent burning. Wash four 1-pint canning jars in hot soapy water; rinse. Prepare 4 lids as manufacturer directs. Fill and cover 1 jar at a time. Pour hot mixture to within 1/4 inch of jar rim. Release trapped air. Wipe rim of jar with a clean damp cloth. Attach lid. Place filled jars in hot water in water-bath canner. Cover all jars with hot water. Bring to a boil. Boil 15 minutes at sea level. Add 1 minute for each 1000 feet of altitude. Remove jars from canner; do not tighten lids. Cool on a rack or on towels in a place free from drafts. Press down on center of lid. If lid is down, seal is completed. If lid goes down as you press, remove ring and tip jar to side to see if there is leakage. Holding edge of lid with several fingers of 1 hand, lift jar 1 inch above table. If lid holds, seal is completed. Refrigerate jars that are not sealed. Label and store sealed jars in a cool dark place. Makes 4 pints.

York State Apple Ketchup

There's more to ketchup than tomatoes. Try this condiment from Colonial days.

1 qt. Apple Base, see below
1 cup sugar
1 tablespoon salt
2 teaspoons ground cinnamon
1 teaspoon ground white pepper

1 teaspoon ground cloves
1 teaspoon dry mustard
2 medium onions, grated
2 cups cider vinegar

Apple Base:
12 Rome Beauty or 15 Granny Smith,
   McIntosh or Wealthy apples

Boiling water

Prepare and measure Apple Base. Pour 4 cups Apple Base into a large saucepan. Stir in sugar, salt, cinnamon, pepper, cloves and mustard until blended. Stir in onions and vinegar. Bring to a boil over medium heat, stirring constantly. Reduce heat to low. Stirring frequently, simmer, uncovered, until thick, 1 hour or more. Pour into 1 or 2 containers with tight-fitting lids. Store in refrigerator up to 2 months. Or, wash two 1-pint canning jars in hot soapy water; rinse. Prepare 2 lids as manufacturer directs. Pour hot mixture into 1 hot jar at a time to within 1/4 inch of jar rim. Release trapped air; wipe rim of jar with a clean damp cloth. Attach lid. Place filled jars in hot water in water-bath canner. Cover all jars with hot water. Bring to a boil. Boil 15 minutes at sea level. Add 1 minute for each 1000 feet of altitude. Remove jars from canner, do not tighten lids. Cool on a rack or on towels in a place free from drafts. Press down on center of lid. If lid is down, seal is completed. If lid goes down as you press, remove ring and tip jar to side to see if there is leakage. Holding edge of lid with several fingers of 1 hand, lift jar 1 inch above table. If lid holds, seal is completed. Refrigerate jars that are not sealed. Label and store sealed jars in a cool dark place. Makes 2 pints.

Apple Base:
Peel and quarter apples. Place in a large saucepan. Add boiling water just to cover apples. Bring to a boil over medium-high heat. Reduce heat to low. Stirring frequently, simmer, uncovered, until all water has evaporated, about 2-1/2 hours. Press through a sieve or food mill.

Kutztown Festival Jam

Spread this Pennsylvania-Dutch treat on hot toast for a wonderful surprise, or serve with chicken or pork.

1/4 cup butter or margarine
2 teaspoons vegetable oil
8 large Bermuda onions, thinly sliced
2 teaspoons salt

1/2 teaspoon ground black pepper
1/4 cup plus 2 tablespoons
   packed brown sugar

In a large heavy skillet, heat butter or margarine with oil over medium-high heat. Add onions. Cook until just beginning to brown, about 10 minutes. Reduce heat to low. Stir in salt and pepper. Partially cover skillet. Cook, stirring frequently, until onions turn caramel color and are very soft, about 30 minutes. Watch carefully to prevent burning. Remove from heat. Stir in sugar until dissolved. Serve hot or cold. Store, covered, in refrigerator up to 4 weeks. Makes about 6 cups.

Cantaloupe Mustard   Photo on page 146.

Lively accompaniment to pork, ham, corned beef and any kind of sausage.

2 (3-1/2-oz.) jars mustard seeds
1 (4-oz.) can or jar dry mustard (1/2 cup)
2 cups boiling water
2 small or 1 large cantaloupe
   (1-1/2 cups pureed pulp)
1 qt. cider vinegar
1 small onion, minced

1/4 cup packed dark-brown sugar
1 teaspoon dried leaf tarragon, crumbled
1 teaspoon dried dillweed
2 teaspoons ground allspice
1-1/2 teaspoons salt
3 tablespoons light corn syrup

In a medium bowl, combine mustard seeds and dry mustard. Pour in boiling water. Let stand, uncovered, at room temperature, 24 hours. Process in blender or food processor until smooth. Pour into a large saucepan. Cut melon in half. Remove seeds and stringy pulp. Peel fruit and cut into large dice. Process in blender or food processor, in convenient amounts, until smooth. Measure 1-1/2 cups pureed cantaloupe. Add to mustard mixture. Stir in vinegar, onion, sugar, tarragon, dillweed, allspice and salt. Bring to a boil over medium-high heat. Reduce heat to low. Stirring frequently, simmer, uncovered, until mixture is very thick, 1 hour or more. Press mixture through a fine sieve. Stir in corn syrup. Pour into a 5-cup container with a tight-fitting lid. Cool. Cover and store in refrigerator up to 2 months. Makes about 5 cups.

Sweet & Savory Mustard

Serve with pork or lamb, or mix it half-and-half with yogurt for a superior dip.

1 cup white-wine vinegar
2 eggs
2 (4-oz.) cans or jars dry mustard (1 cup)

1 teaspoon salt
2/3 cup packed dark-brown sugar
1/4 teaspoon ground turmeric

In blender or food processor, combine all ingredients. Process until smooth and blended. Pour into top of a double boiler. Stir constantly over simmering water until thickened, about 5 minutes. Cool 10 minutes. Spoon into a 1-pint jar with a tight-fitting cover. Cover and store in refrigerator up to 4 weeks. Makes about 2 cups.

If you make jelly at home, enhance some of each batch with herbs: simply place a sprig of the chosen herb into the glass before pouring in the hot liquid. Tarragon is excellent with apple jelly, thyme with grape, rosemary with orange, mint with red currant, marjoram with strawberry or raspberry.

How to Make Cantaloupe Mustard

1/Peel fruit; cut into large dice. Process in blender or food processor, in convenient amounts, until smooth.

2/Add pureed cantaloupe and remaining spices to mustard mixture. Cook until thick; press through a fine sieve.

Spiced Currants

Serve hot or cold as an unusual condiment with meat or poultry dishes.

1 (16-oz.) pkg. dried currants
   (3-1/3 cups)
2 cups packed light-brown sugar
3/4 cup red-wine vinegar

3/4 cup water
1-1/2 teaspoons ground cinnamon
1/2 teaspoon ground cloves

Wash and pick over currants to remove stems or foreign matter. In a medium saucepan, combine sugar, vinegar and water. Stir over medium heat until sugar is dissolved. Reduce heat to low. Simmer 5 minutes. Add currants, cinnamon and cloves. Bring to a boil over medium-high heat. Reduce heat to low. Stirring occasionally, simmer, uncovered, 15 minutes. Serve currants drained or with a small amount of their liquid. Or, pour into a container with a tight-fitting lid. Cover and store in refrigerator up to 4 weeks. Makes about 2-1/2 cups.

Hidden Farm Pickled Crab Apples

Chubby little sweet-tart-spicy accompaniments to poultry, pork or game.

4 qts. whole crab apples (about 6 lbs.)	**1/2 teaspoon salt**
3 cups cider vinegar	**1 tablespoon mixed pickling spices**
1 cup water	**1 tablespoon whole cloves**
6 cups sugar	**1 (5-inch) cinnamon stick, broken**

Wash seven 1-pint canning jars in hot soapy water; rinse. Keep hot until needed. Prepare lids as manufacturer directs. Remove blossom ends of crab apples. Do not remove stem ends. In a large pot, combine vinegar, water, sugar and salt. In a square of cheesecloth that will accommodate them loosely, place pickling spices, cloves and cinnamon. Tie into a bag with string. Add to vinegar mixture. Bring to a boil, stirring until sugar is dissolved. Add about 6 cups crab apples. Cook until tender but still firm, about 15 minutes. With a skimmer or slotted spoon, fill hot jars with crab apples; keep hot in hot-water bath. Add another 6 cups crab apples to vinegar solution. Repeat cooking and filling jars until all crab apples are used. Remove spice bag from liquid. Bring liquid to a boil. Fill and cover 1 jar at a time. Pour hot liquid over crab apples to within 1/4 inch of rim. Release trapped air. Wipe rim of jar with a clean damp cloth. Attach lid. Place filled jars in hot water in water-bath canner. Cover all jars with hot water. Bring to a boil. Boil 15 minutes at sea level. Add 1 minute for each 1000 feet of altitude. Remove jars from canner; do not tighten lids. Cool on a rack or on towels in a place free from drafts. Press down on center of lid. If lid is down, seal is completed. If lid goes down as you press, remove ring and tip jar to side to see if there is leakage. Holding edge of lid with several fingers of 1 hand, lift jar 1 inch above table. If lid holds, seal is completed. Refrigerate jars that are not sealed. Label and store sealed jars in a cool dark place. Makes about 7 pints.

Holiday Cranberry Conserve

Easy enough to make so you'll want to serve it on any festive occasion.

1 (1-lb.) pkg. fresh or frozen cranberries	**1 cup chopped walnuts**
2 cups sugar	**1/4 teaspoon ground cloves**
1 cup cold water	**1 cup orange juice**
1 tablespoon grated orange peel	**1 cup chopped celery**
1 cup golden raisins	**1 medium apple, peeled, chopped**
1 teaspoon ground ginger	

In a large heavy saucepan, combine cranberries and sugar. Stir in water. Over medium heat, bring to a boil, stirring frequently. Reduce heat to low. Simmer, uncovered, 15 minutes. Remove from heat. Stir in remaining ingredients. Let stand at room temperature 20 minutes. Spoon into a container or jar with a tight-fitting lid. Cover and store in refrigerator up to 2 weeks. Makes 7 cups.

Green-Tomato Preserve

A happy choice to accompany almost any meat main dish, especially in cold weather.

12 cups coarsely chopped green tomatoes
   (about 5-1/2 lbs.)
1 lb. light-brown sugar
2 cups cider vinegar
1 tablespoon salt
1 large onion, chopped

1 tablespoon curry powder
2-1/2 teaspoons ground allspice
2-1/2 teaspoons mustard seeds
1-1/2 teaspoons ground ginger
1 teaspoon ground cumin
1 teaspoon coarsely ground black pepper

In large pot or Dutch oven, combine tomatoes, sugar and vinegar. Cook over low heat, stirring frequently, until sugar dissolves. Stir in remaining ingredients. Simmer, stirring frequently to prevent burning, until thickened, 1-1/2 to 2 hours. Ladle into several containers with tight-fitting lids. Cool. Cover and store in refrigerator up to 6 weeks. Or, wash three 1-pint canning jars in hot soapy water; rinse. Keep hot until needed. Prepare 3 lids as manufacturer directs. Fill and cover 1 jar at a time. Pour hot mixture to within 1/4 inch of jar rim. Release trapped air. Wipe rim of jar with a clean damp cloth. Attach lid. Place filled jars in hot water in water-bath canner. Cover all jars with hot water. Bring to a boil. Boil 10 minutes at sea level. Add 1 minute for each 1000 feet of altitude. Remove jars from canner; do not tighten lids. Cool on a rack or on towels in a place free from drafts. Press down on center of lid. If lid is down, seal is completed. If lid goes down as you press, remove ring and tip jar to side to see if there is leakage. Holding edge of lid with several fingers of 1 hand, lift jar 1 inch above table. If lid holds, seal is completed. Refrigerate jars that are not sealed. Label and store sealed jars in a cool dark place. Makes 3 pints.

Shaker Baked Applesauce

Sauce for breakfast or lunch, condiment with pork or ham, dessert with whipped cream.

8 lbs. tart cooking apples, quartered
1 cup water
1 cup packed light-brown sugar
2 teaspoons ground cinnamon
1 teaspoon ground nutmeg

1/2 teaspoon ground cloves
1/2 teaspoon salt
About 1 cup granulated sugar
1 tablespoon grated orange peel
1 cup coarsely chopped walnuts

Place apples in a large pot or Dutch oven. Add water. Bring to a boil over medium-high heat. Reduce heat to low. Stirring occasionally, simmer, uncovered, until apples are soft, 10 to 25 minutes. Press through a food mill or sieve, removing as much pulp as possible. Preheat oven to 300F (150C). Pour apple pulp into a 4-quart baking pan. Stir in brown sugar, cinnamon, nutmeg, cloves, salt and 1 cup granulated sugar. Taste and add more granulated sugar, if desired. Bake, uncovered, in preheated oven 1-1/2 hours, stirring 3 times. Stir in orange peel and walnuts. Bake 30 minutes longer, stirring once. Cool to room temperature. Spoon into containers with tight-fitting lids. Cover and store in refrigerator up to 2 weeks. Makes 8 to 9 cups.

Mail-Order Sources for Spices, Herbs & Other Seasoning & Flavoring Agents

Local supermarkets and specialty stores may not offer all you want in the way of seasonings and flavorings. You may want some exotic things that few retailers stock. If so, turn to the mail to bring you just what you need. Here are some reliable mail-order houses that specialize in foodstuffs and kitchenwares. Most of them have catalogs. Some are free; some are sold at a small price which is refunded with the first order. Write and inquire about the specific products you have in mind. You'll get a catalog or ordering information in return.

Aphrodesia Products
28 Carmine Street
New York, NY 10014
Wide variety of spices and herbs.

Balducci's
424 Avenue of the Americas
New York, NY 10011
Olive oil, seasoned oils, vinegars, epicurean specialties.

Bon Appétit Gourmet Foods
84 Higuera Street
Culver City, CA 90230
Wide variety of herbs and spices, flavored vinegars and oils, mustards, spreads, many interesting gourmet foods.

Casados Farms
P.O. Box 1269
San Juan Pueblo, NM 87566
Wide variety of chili peppers, whole dried and ground.

Cedars Import Co.
2606 South Sheridan
Tulsa, OK 74129
Eastern Indian and Mid-Eastern spices and seasonings.

The Cuisine Marketplace
133B West De La Guerra
Santa Barbara, CA 93101
Wide variety of spices and herbs, a guidebook to herbs, spices and essential oils, many kitchen tools and gadgets.

Dri Harvest Foods, Ltd.
2434 80th Avenue
Edmonton, Alberta
Canada
Standard and imported spices and herbs.

Gazin
Box 19221
2910 Toulouse Street
New Orleans, LA 70179
Creole, Cajun and Acadian herbs, spices and seasonings, foods, tools, gadgets.

Horticultural Enterprises
P.O. Box 340082
Dallas, TX 75234
Seeds for over 25 varieties of home-grown chili peppers.

House of Rice
4112 University Way NE
Seattle, WA 98105
Indonesian, Chinese, Philippine and Japanese foods and seasonings.

Kitchen Bazaar
4455 Connecticut Avenue N. W.
Washington, DC 20008
Herbs, spices, tools, gadgets, usual and unusual housewares, cookbooks, full line of home-kitchen utensils.

Paprikás Weiss
1546 Second Avenue
New York, NY 10028
Spices, herbs and seasonings (including variety of paprikas), flavoring extracts, imported specialties, cookwares.

Pecos River Spice Co.
P.O. Box 680B
New York, NY 10021
Ingredients for Southwestern and Mexican foods.

Rafal Spice Co.
2521 Russell
Detroit, MI 48207
Wide variety of spices, herbs, seasonings and extracts.

H. Roth & Son
1577 First Avenue
New York, NY 10028
Spices, herbs, grains, wide variety of coffees and teas, tools, gadgets, unusual cookware.

Select Origins
670 West End Avenue, Suite 10E
New York, NY 10025
Imported and domestic spices, herbs and seasonings.

Spice of Life
600 Miller Valley Road
Prescott, AZ 66301
Spices, herbs, seasonings, blends, tea blends and more.

Taylor's Herb Gardens Inc.
1535 Lone Oak Road
Vista, CA 92083
Herb seeds and live herb plants, with planting instructions.

Tia Mia
P. O. Box 685
Sunland Park, NM 88063
Wide variety of chilies and chili foods.

Watkins
150 Liberty Street
Winona, MN 55987
Wide variety of spices, herbs and flavoring extracts.

Index

Index

Index

Index

8.32746901373